THE QUEEN'S DAUGHTERS IN INDIA

First published 1899
This edition published by Lector House in 2024

ISBN: 978-93-6138-707-4

Lector House LLP
Registered Office: H. No. 96, Block C, Tomar Colony,
Burari, Delhi – 110084, India
info@lectorhouse.com
www.lectorhouse.com

THE QUEEN'S DAUGHTERS IN INDIA

ELIZABETH W. ANDREW,
KATHARINE CAROLINE BUSHNELL

2024

LECTOR HOUSE LLP

THE QUEEN'S DAUGHTERS IN INDIA.

BY

ELIZABETH W. ANDREW
AND
KATHARINE C. BUSHNELL.

WITH PREFATORY LETTERS BY
MRS. JOSEPHINE E. BUTLER
AND
MR. HENRY J. WILSON, M.P.

"Remember them that are in bonds as bound with them."

DEDICATED
TO
JOSEPHINE E. BUTLER,

PROPHETESS OF THE TRUTH IN CHRIST JESUS; LOVER OF HOLY JUSTICE; FRIEND OF OUTCAST WOMEN; LEADER OF "THE NEW ABOLITIONISTS"; WHOM GOD HATH ANOINTED WITH HIS OWN PECULIAR JOY. BECAUSE, IN THE SPIRIT OF HER MASTER, SHE HATH "LOVED RIGHTEOUSNESS AND HATED INIQUITY."

PREFACE TO THE FIRST EDITION.

THIS little book is written under a deep sense of obligation to the womanhood of the world, but more especially under a sense of duty to God. A group of women of the British aristocracy have lifted their voices in advocacy of licensed vice; and their sycophants and admirers in England and America are either re-echoing their plea or excusing their conduct. The plea is made primarily for India, but incidentally for all Christendom, and every effort is being put forth, openly or covertly, to contaminate public sentiment on this point.

In five States of America, in a little over a year, the attempt has been made to secure legislation for the compulsory periodical examination of women; and a strong organization exists on both sides of the water to promote this infamous object. Under these conditions it is a matter of grave moment that certain secular, temperance, and religious periodicals which would have sounded a clear note of warning six months ago, are today being deceived. They print the outrageous falsehoods that represent India as having become a menace to the health of England because of the abolition of brothel slavery in that country. Excuses are made for the shallow-brained sophistry of those who pretend that the compulsory periodical examination of women can be divorced from the moral debasement of women, and as though such compulsory examination were something quite unlike the notorious Contagious Diseases Acts. High titles and famous names are quoted as a warrant for advocating the iniquity; and certain men are being exalted as though famous temperance advocates, who are not themselves total abstainers, and who are well-known public advocates of licensed fornication. Thus is introduced into philanthropic movements of the present day an element of fatal moral confusion, as though a person who boldly defies the principles of ordinary decency in one direction could be received as a trusted and efficient promoter of decency along another line; as though a man could be relied upon as an advocate and apostle of that of which he is not an example. We do not doubt that some of the persons who do these things are well-intentioned; but they expend their benevolence on the wolf and forget the lamb. They would win others to play with them on the asp's nest.

We have determined on our knees before God that those who advocate the compulsory periodical examination of women shall do so knowing what it means, and knowing also that their friends and neighbours understand what is being advocated.

We offer no apology for our plainness of speech; to employ smooth language and obscure phrases in the present crisis would be to trifle with a deadly enemy—

to toy with the Indian cobra.

September, 1897.

FROM MRS. JOSEPHINE E. BUTLER.

I wish that every woman in the United Kingdom could read this little book. It tells the truth, the terrible truth, concerning the treatment of certain Indian women, our fellow-citizens and sisters, by the British Government. I believe if that truth were known throughout the length and breadth of our land, it would become impossible for our rulers to continue to maintain the cruel and wicked Regulations by which these Indian women are enslaved and destroyed.

I am a loyal Englishwoman; I love my country. It is because of my great love for her that I mourn so deeply over her dishonour in the promotion of such legislation and practices as this book exposes, and that I will not cease to denounce the crimes committed in her name so long as I have life and breath.

I thank God that the writers of this book have been raised up to plead the sacred cause of Justice and of Womanhood; and I rejoice to know that God has bestowed on them a measure of the fearless spirit of the faithful prophets and prophetesses of old, to rebuke national sin and to preach repentance to the people.

JOSEPHINE E. BUTLER.

Feb. 1898.

FROM MR. HENRY J. WILSON, M.P.

Dear Friends,

I am glad you intend to reprint "The Queen's Daughters in India."

It brings home to many who will never read Blue Books the terrible facts about officially-authorized vice; and it shows the moral aspects of the "Regulation" system, which Blue Books never show.

I remember very clearly how your first Report, in 1892, of what you had seen, impressed us all as a very careful record of a very careful investigation.

Then, in 1893, I was a member of the Departmental Committee appointed to hear your evidence, when your clear testimony, which no cross-examination could shake, gave abundant evidence of your close observation and the accuracy of your records.

The impression this made on me was only deepened when, in India, in 1894 (on the Opium Commission), I saw one of the places you had described with such remarkable closeness of detail.

It is deplorable that we should have to fight this battle again. But so it is. Princesses and Titled Ladies have added their influence to that of the panic-mongering materialists, in the endeavour to "make the practice of prostitution, if not absolutely innocuous, at least, much less dangerous"—for that is, in the language of the Royal Commissioners of 1871, the object in view.

I thank God, therefore, that you are able to visit this country again, to help us both by voice and pen in the renewed agitation which is forced upon us.

Yours faithfully,
Henry J. Wilson.

Feb., 1898.

CONTENTS

Page

Dedication vi

Preface to the First Edition. vii

From Mrs. Josephine E. Butler. ix

From Mr. Henry J. Wilson, M.P. x

I. Cantonment Life in India. 1

II. Seeking the Outcast. 11

III. The Habitations of Cruelty. 19

IV. The Contagious Diseases Acts. 29

V. Pleading for the Oppressed. 41

VI. Some Anglo-Indian Moral Sentiments. 49

Appendices. 57

THE QUEEN'S DAUGHTERS IN INDIA.

I.

CANTONMENT LIFE IN INDIA.

A GENTLEMAN in India, who had spent many years in military service, told us the following tradition:—

"In the year 1856, before the Mutiny, Lady —— was one evening riding out on horseback at Umballa, unattended, when the bridle of her horse was suddenly seized by a British soldier who was possessed of evil designs against her. Most earnestly she protested against his violence, and remonstrated with him that, besides the wrong to her, to injure one of her social rank would utterly ruin his entire future, as he would be flogged and dismissed from the army in disgrace. Thereupon ensued a conversation in which he pleaded extenuation for such a crime so successfully that she readily accepted his false statement that there was excuse for vice when soldiers were not allowed to marry. After that experience she sought opportunity to talk with high military officials concerning the necessity of protecting high-born ladies from such risks, by furnishing opportunities for sensual indulgence to the British soldiers, and the result was the elaboration and extension of a system for the apportionment of native women to regiments." We have never been able to verify the exact truth of this incident, but it probably has a basis in fact. Yet it has had its counterpart in a recent movement among the aristocratic women of England to re-introduce the same wicked legislation. It is on this account that the authors have considered it necessary to print a more extended account of the work in behalf of the women of India, in which they have had a large share. If the exceedingly simple style in which they give their story seems to some readers almost an insult to their intelligence, and lacking in the delicacy of touch that could be desired, it must not be forgotten for one moment that they are writing with special regard for those in the humblest ranks of life, who have often had scant opportunities for education; for it is upon the daughters of such that the oppressive laws for the licensing of prostitution fall; and in large part the supposed advantages of licensed prostitution accrue to the upper social classes, which are, in fact, the lower moral classes. The crusade against licensed fornication is a war between respectable daughters of the poor and rich and powerful men and women.

Whether the narrative given above be wholly true or not, the fact remains that when so-called "Christian England" took control of "heathen India," and plots of ground called Cantonments were staked off for the residence of the British soldiers and their officers, full provision was made for the flesh, to fulfil the lusts thereof. A Cantonment is a considerable section of land, sometimes comprising several square miles; and within these Cantonments much more arbitrary law prevails than the civil law by which the rest of the country is governed. There are about one hundred military Cantonments in India. Sometimes these Cantonments have few inhabitants besides the soldiers and a few traders in groceries, etc., for the soldiers; and again in some places a whole city has grown up within the Cantonment, and many Europeans reside therein, feeling more safe in case of threatened trouble from an uprising of the people against the Government, than outside under civil law only. All the land of a Cantonment belongs to the Government, and in case of war the military officials may seize, for residence, all the houses within the Cantonment without regard to the actual owners of the buildings, and the commanding officer has the power of expelling any one he pleases from the Cantonment, without assigning any reason for so doing.

The system devised for furnishing sensual indulgence to the British soldier, and for protecting him from diseases consequent on such indulgence, was commonly called the Contagious Diseases Acts, but was carried out under Cantonment Regulations, and was as follows in its main features:—

There were placed with each regiment (of about a thousand soldiers) from twelve to fifteen native women, who dwelt in appointed houses or tents, as the case might be, called "chaklas." These women were allowed to consort with British soldiers only, and were registered by the Cantonment magistrate, and tickets of license were given them.

Besides the "chakla," *i.e.*, the Government brothel, there was in each Cantonment a prison hospital, in which the patients were confined against their will. To these Lock Hospitals the women were obliged to go periodically (generally once a week) for an indecent examination, to see whether every part of the body was free from any trace of diseases likely to spread from them to the soldiers, as the result of immoral relations. The compulsory examination is in itself a surgical rape. When a woman was found diseased, she was detained in the hospital until cured; when found healthy she was given a ticket of license to practise fornication and was returned to the chakla for that purpose.

In case a woman tried to escape from the chakla, or from the Lock Hospital, and was apprehended, she would be taken to the Cantonment magistrate, who would punish her with fine or imprisonment.

Even the price of the visits of soldiers to the chakla was fixed by military usage, and was so low that the soldier would scarcely miss what he expended in vicious indulgence. We have frequently heard in England that the officers sent out in the English towns to secure recruits for the army hold out, as an inducement to young men to enlist, the fact that a licentious life in India is so cheap, and that the Government will see to it that no disease will follow the soldiers' profligacy. But this last promise is altogether false, for statistics show that with all their efforts diseases increase with the increase of licentiousness, with small regard to the military surgeons' efforts to make it physically safe.

When a regiment came into a large Cantonment where there were barracks, there was generally a large Government brothel to which all the women were sent for residence, and a guard in uniform looked after them. When the soldiers were camped out in the open field, tents were set up for the women at the back part of the encampment. When the soldiers marched, the women were carried in carts, with British soldiers to guard them, or sent by train to the destination of the regiment. In charge of the women was placed a superintendent or brothel-keeper, called the "mahaldarni." She also was expected to procure women as desired; and we have ourselves read the official permits granted these women to go out to procure more women when needed.

On June 17, 1886, a military order, known among the opponents of State regulation as the "Infamous Circular Memorandum," was sent to all the Cantonments of India by Quartermaster-General Chapman, in the name of the Commander-in-Chief of the army in India (Lord Roberts). But during the course of the enquiry of the Departmental Committee of 1893, its real author was discovered to be Lord Roberts himself, not his Quartermaster-General.

This Memorandum (Parliamentary Paper No. 197, of 1888) is a lengthy document, every part of which has painful interest; but we can only give a faint outline. It specified certain measures to be instituted as means for looking more carefully after the health of British soldiers, and the observations therein were to be heeded by the "military and medical authorities in every command" throughout India. (See Appendix A.)

This order said (and military orders are well-nigh inexorable): "In the regimental bazaars[1] it is necessary to have a sufficient number of women, to take care that they are sufficiently attractive, to provide them with proper houses, and, above all, to insist upon means of ablution being always available." It proceeds: "If young soldiers are carefully advised in regard to the advantage of ablution, and recognise that convenient arrangements exist in the regimental bazaar [that is, in the chakla], they may be expected to avoid the risks involved in association with women who are not recognised [that is, licensed] by the regimental authorities." In other words, young soldiers are not expected to be moral, but only to be instructed as to the safest way of practising immorality. This remarkable document goes on to suggest that young soldiers should be taught to consider it a "point of honour" to save each other from contagion by pointing out to their officers women with whom there was risk of disease. The document calls attention to the need of more women, and the necessity of making the free quarters "houses that will meet the wishes of the women"—in order, it is implied, that they may be the more easily lured to live in them.

The official record of what followed, as a result of effort on the part of under-officials to carry out the instructions of the Commander-in-Chief (Lord Roberts) is truly shocking, as might be expected. The officer in command of the 2nd Battalion Cheshire Regiment sent the following application to the magistrate of Umballa Cantonment: "Requisition for extra attractive women for regimental bazaar, in accordance with Circular Memorandum 21a." "These women's fares," it continues, "by one-horse conveyances, from Umballa to Solon, will be paid by the Cheshire Regiment on arrival. Please send young and attractive women, as laid

[1] Trading-posts for the supply of necessaries to the soldiers; but the author means, in explicit terms, the chakla or brothel.

down in Quartermaster-General's Circular, No. 21a." Then he added a note to the effect that some of the women already at hand were not very attractive, adding: "Application has been made to the Cantonment magistrate of Umballa for others, but up to date none have arrived; therefore, it is presumed a great difficulty exists in procuring the class of young women asked for." Evidently it was an amazing thing to these self-styled Christian military officials that heathen women would not flock to their slave pens!

Another commanding officer writes: "There are not enough women; they are not attractive enough. More and younger women are required, and their houses should be improved." Yet another commanding officer writes: "I have ordered the number of prostitutes to be increased to twelve, and have given special instructions as to the four additional women being young and of attractive appearance."

Such was the zeal for increasing the facilities for safe vice, provoked by such military methods as described by this Memorandum, that the unwillingness of the native women to plunge into a life of shame at the behest of their conquerors, received scant consideration. A retired soldier, living at Lucknow, told us of his own observations a few years before: that, if a native policeman saw a young girl talking indiscreetly, though innocently, with a man, he would denounce her as a suspected prostitute; she would be brought before the Cantonment magistrate, and be registered to live among the soldiers. He said the police made large sums of money by threatening to thus hand over girls to the magistrate, and demanding bribes as the alternative of such a horrible fate. A Christian Englishman, holding a responsible position under the Government, vouched for by the Editor of the *Bombay Guardian*, relates what he saw in four Cantonments, where the instructions of the "Infamous Memorandum" were carried out, in the following language:—

> "The orders specified were faithfully carried out, under the supervision of commanding officers, and were to this effect. The commanding officer gave orders to his quartermaster to arrange with the regimental *Kutwal* [an under-official, native] to take two policemen (without uniform), and go into the villages and take from the homes of these poor people their daughters from fourteen years and upwards, about twelve or fifteen girls at a time. They were to select the best-looking. Next morning, these were all put in front of the Colonel and Quartermaster. The former made his selection of the number required. They were then presented with a pass or license, and then made over to the old woman in charge of this house of vice under the Government. The women already there, who were examined by the doctor, and found diseased, had their passes taken away from them, and were then removed by the police out of the Cantonment, and these fresh, innocent girls put in their places."

There is a whole volume of misery expressed in that last sentence, both for the fresh, innocent girls, and for the diseased ones turned out of the Cantonment. It has been repeatedly asserted that this system of regulating vice was so merciful, even to the girls; for their diseases, it has been claimed, were never allowed to go beyond the initial stage. But what this witness states is strictly in accordance with what we found to be the case. When we visited some of these Lock Hospitals and examined the records kept there, we noted that in the annual reports no cases of secondary stages of disease were mentioned; but when we questioned the native physicians in charge as to whether these ever arose, they answered that frequently such cases occurred, but when a woman became unfit to practise prostitution, because of that fact, she was turned out of the Cantonment.

The British officials of India have not shown the slightest concern as to the spread of disease, even when introduced by their own race among the natives, but have actually sent these women abroad to scatter disease wherever they go. And what can a poor Army slave-woman do when thus turned out? Her caste is broken, because she has lived with foreigners, and her friends will seldom receive her back; she has been compelled to follow the soldiers on the march; and when dismissed may be hundreds of miles away from any human being who ever saw her face before. Practically almost every industrial door in India is closed to women, the nurse-girl to foreign children being so exceptional as not worthy of mention among the hundreds of millions of people. The Cantonment sometimes includes all there is of city life in the whole region, and the woman has no choice but the open fields or the jungle. God alone knows the fate of these helpless creatures, and few beside care to know.

This was the exact state of things, with details too infamous to commit to paper, until 1886, when the Contagious Diseases Acts which had prevailed in the military stations of England were repealed as the result of a remarkable crusade led by Mrs. Josephine Butler. As the dependencies of Great Britain are all supposed to be governed by the same policy as that of England, the repeal of the Contagious Diseases Acts there virtually repealed them in India. But it was not until 1888 that a despatch was sent to India by the Secretary of State for India, whose duty it is to attend to such matters, declaring that the system was "indefensible, and must be condemned."

A copy of Lord Roberts' "Infamous Memorandum" fell into the hands of a Christian gentleman who sent it to England. It was there reprinted and distributed to every member of the House of Commons, and created a great sensation, meeting with almost universal condemnation. Following upon the popular indignation created thereby, the House of Commons on June 5, 1888, passed a unanimous resolution that "Any mere suspension of measures for the compulsory examination of women, and for licensing and regulating prostitution in India, is insufficient; and the legislation which enjoins, authorizes, or permits such measures ought to be repealed."

The publication of the "Infamous Memorandum" in England had shown that the existing Indian Cantonment Acts must be condemned, and they were superseded by rules made under a new law, the "Cantonments Act of 1889." This was a very specious document, which avoided the issue by merely placing unlimited powers in the hands of the Governor-General in Council to "make rules consistent with this Act, for the prevention of the spread of infectious and contagious disorders within the Cantonment."

It was so recognised and pronounced upon by the newspapers of India, which favoured licensed vice. Commenting on the new Cantonments Act one newspaper said: "The religious fanatics who howled until a weak Government gave way to their clamour . . . will probably howl again now at the way the old order of things will be enforced under another name, but with very little difference in manner." Another said: "Their phraseology is the work of a master in the art of making a thing look as unlike itself as it well can be." Many others spoke in the same strain. Immediately the advocates of the abolition of licensed prostitution took alarm, and began a vigorous remonstrance; for they saw great danger in any law which put large discretionary power into the hands of officials. The late Rt. Hon. Sir James Stansfeld, M.P., and Professor Stuart, M.P., addressed a letter to the Secretary of State for India concerning this new Act, in which they said, among other things: "If our interpretation of the new proposed regulations is correct, they may be used to set up again a system of compulsory examination of prostitutes, and to regulate and license, within the Cantonment, the calling of those prostitutes who submit to periodical examination, and to certify and license those who are pronounced physically fit."

The official reply from the Secretary of State for India was to the effect that the Home Government was unwilling to believe, without positive proof, that this new Cantonments Act would be used to foster licensed prostitution.

It should be explained here that Abolitionists have always recognised that to establish the periodical examination is, in and of itself, to license prostitution; for there can be no possible excuse for the reiterated examination of healthy women, in anticipation of possible contagion, without recognising a certain right to practise prostitution, if the women be pronounced medically "fit" for such a calling. The periodical examination of women, then, constitutes the living heart of all those forms of legislation generally comprised under the term, "The Contagious Diseases Acts," by whatever local name such regulations may be known.

We came to England in the winter of 1890–91, it being the first country visited by us on a round-the-world journey for the World's W.C.T.U., with which we were, at that time, officially connected.[2]

During this visit we frequently met and talked with Mrs. Josephine Butler, known and revered by lovers of purity throughout the world for her heroic service in the cause of the Abolition of State Regulation of Vice. She expressed a strong desire that while in India in the course of our journey we should make a careful investigation into the conditions prevailing there, and learn, if possible, whether the resolution of the House of Commons of June 5, 1888, was being obeyed. As already noted, this resolution demanded the repeal of all measures that enjoined, authorized, or permitted the compulsory examination of women and the licensing and regulation of prostitution. It was desired also that we should secure for the use of Parliamentary members of the British Committee of the Federation for the Abolition of State Regulation of Vice actual proof that the resolution was being disobeyed, such as would meet the official demand for proof from the Secretary of State, before he would be willing to believe that the new Cantonments Act was

[2] We resigned June 15, 1896.

being used to foster licensed prostitution. The mission was pronounced by Mrs. Butler "one of the most difficult and even perilous missions ever undertaken in the course of our great crusade." After due consideration and prayer for guidance, we consented to undertake the task.

The British Committee of the Federation furnished us with all necessary official documents with which to make ourselves thoroughly conversant with the history of the C. D. Acts throughout the British dependencies in the Orient, and supplied us with a letter of introduction to a staunch friend of the cause in India, with whom we were expected to hold frequent consultations.

We took our departure from England in the month of July, 1891, going first of all to South Africa and labouring in the interests of our work there until the cold season set in and we could proceed to India. Reaching India at the end of December, 1891, we conveyed our letter of introduction to this confidential friend, who advised us to proceed northward and consult with a friend of the cause who understood thoroughly the interior life of the people, and, it was believed, would give great aid to our mission. Travelling northward we arrived at the station designated, and sought an interview with this gentleman.

We intimated to him what we hoped to accomplish in India, with a view to obtaining an expression from him of his willingness to aid us. With consternation and embarrassment he protested against our undertaking anything so foolish and impracticable, declaring from his long experience that it was utterly impossible for women to get at the truth, and entreating us to abandon so wild a project. When he saw that we did not yield the matter, he questioned us as to what we were planning to do, how we should proceed to get information in a country whose customs and language were so utterly unknown to us, and concerning a military system with which, as Americans, we were quite unacquainted. We withheld further confidence, simply saying with earnestness, "Whether this is practicable or impracticable, women have a right to this knowledge; and we do not think it foolish or impracticable to trust God to give us all the information we need, without human aid."

He felt the most kindly interest in us personally, and manifested this by several practical expressions; but doubtless he reasoned that he could not encourage us in what he believed to be an impossible undertaking.

This experience drove us to God, our only helper. We were strangers in a strange land, carrying the burden of a sacred secret which weighed us to the earth. After much prayer and deliberation we called on the chief military surgeon in charge of the station hospital of —— Cantonment. This official began almost immediately when we called upon him, and entirely without suggestion from us, to deplore "the repeal of the C. D. Acts," and, as he claimed, the consequent increase of specific diseases. He showed us his daily report, which illustrated what he said on this subject. These diseases, he said, were for the most part contracted on the march or in the hills, especially at Ranikhet. This interview took place on January 4, 1892.

The surgeon said he wondered that people did not, from the moral and religious point of view, see the injury that the repeal of the Contagious Diseases Acts was doing, not only to the soldiers but to the whole country; "and," he added, "we can do nothing." We asked, "Is there, then, no form of regulation now?" He answered emphatically, "*None whatever.*" He said, "We can do nothing about the women outside the Cantonment, and there is the trouble." He added, "Those inside go on as they used to, and go to the hospital for treatment when diseased. But," he continued in an aggrieved tone, "this is absolutely voluntary; we have no control."

He said there was a European physician in charge of the hospital, to whom he had just been talking regarding the matter when we came in. We said, "There is a European physician in charge, then, is there?" He answered, "Yes; but the hospital is not for these diseases only, but also for fevers, dysentery, cholera, and all diseases"; and that there were men there as well as women. We asked, "Is the Lock Hospital, then, entirely disused?" He replied, "Why, there is *no* Lock Hospital." He added that many good people were getting their eyes opened now as to the condition of things, and that even some clergymen had the courage of their moral convictions, and had come out in favour of the Contagious Diseases Acts.

Previous to leaving England we had received information concerning this Cantonment and its Lock Hospital. Our information, compared with this official's inconsistent statements, convinced us that he was endeavouring to mislead us. After other and many futile efforts to reach the truth, we gave ourselves up wholly to prayer, remembering the promise, "They shall come with weeping, and with supplications will I lead them. I will cause them to walk by the rivers of waters in a straight way, wherein they shall not stumble." We felt sure that any mistake at the outset of our work, such as giving confidence to the wrong person, or any indiscreet action that might betray our object in visiting India, would be fatal to our purpose; therefore we cried to God to preserve us from impatience and to keep our feet from stumbling.

We went next to Agra and remained there several days, wandering about the old fort and other places of interest. But surely never was sadder sight-seeing! The way seemed utterly closed against us. The work stretched, vast and difficult, before us, and those towering thick walls that surround the fort, with a deep moat at their foot, represented to our thoughts the pride, strength, and secrecy of the system which we sought to penetrate, and at other times the barriers that separated us from the enslaved women whom we had come to India in the hope of helping.

Nearly five weeks had gone by; the winter season was rapidly passing, and we were yet without a single clue to guide us in our investigations.

One Sunday we set apart for fasting and prayer—in the morning instructing the native servants at the Rest House where we were staying to leave us uninterrupted until the evening, as it was a sacred day with us, and we wished to be alone. We locked our doors and waited on the Father of spirits for guidance. Never shall we forget the hours of that day. At the beginning our hearts seemed completely crushed under a sense of our absolute helplessness and ignorance; but we know now that we were in the very place of power—that it was only there that

God could reveal Himself to our waiting spirits. It was at the first, however, inexpressibly dark. Still we held on, in faith that light would come; and before night, light was fully given to us both, as to our next step, which was that we were to go to a friend in a neighbouring city and lay the whole case before her. We obeyed the guidance; and although our friend was exceedingly hopeless as to our undertaking, yet she was willing to give us the assistance of her quick intelligence and long acquaintance with India. She proved of invaluable service to us in teaching us many simple colloquial phrases, and inducting us into a knowledge of the customs of the country, thus making us much more independent in our work and travels.

At this time it became clear to us that we must approach the whole question from the native side. We had gained nothing in seeking information from European officials. Our hope now lay in interviewing the native physicians and the women themselves. We did not at first venture to ask the way to the Lock Hospital, taking it for granted that this term had long before fallen into disuse, as the existence of this hospital was officially denied. But after visiting various hospitals within a Cantonment, and failing to find the "Cantonment Hospital" so called, which term we were told was now applied to the place for which we were searching, we asked for the Lock Hospital, and to our surprise found that in common parlance it was still so named. Our cab-drivers always understood instantly what we meant when we used either this term or the native term, which means a hospital for degraded women. Our first actual interview was held with the dhai, or nurse, and inmates of a Lock Hospital. Besides much valuable information gained from them, we learned the native name used to designate the quarters within the military Cantonments for degraded women, viz., "The Chakla."

From this time forward, our way became much more plain, as in the ten Cantonments visited[3] we found that we needed only to give directions to our cabmen and they would take us without hesitation both to the Lock Hospital and to the chakla, these places being perfectly well known to the natives residing within the Cantonment.

These Cantonments are all under military rule. As our work lay only within the Cantonments the military regulations, of course, applied to us. One of these rules made it possible at any time for us to be excluded, for it refers to "persons whom the Commanding Officer deems it expedient to exclude from the Cantonment, with or without assigning any reason for excluding them therefrom" (Cantonments Act, chap. 5, sec. 26, clause 23). It was necessary, therefore, that we should not attract attention to the fact that we were making investigations as to whether the resolution of the House of Commons was being obeyed or not by the military authorities. Had our errand been suspected, we could have been sent out of the Cantonment at once, with no explanation and no opportunity for redress. We therefore proceeded as quietly as possible.

Towards the last our enquiries proceeded very rapidly, for we had learned to accomplish as much in one day as would formerly have occupied a week. The

[3] The Cantonments we visited were Bareilly, Lucknow, Meerut, Lahore (Cantonment Station, Meean Meer), Rawal Pindi, Peshawar, Amritzar, Umballa, Sitapur, and Benares. Five of these we visited a second time.

winter season was over, and we were now in the month of March, with the heat of the advancing Indian summer daily increasing in terrible force, and becoming oppressive to our unaccustomed Anglo-Saxon constitutions. We travelled by night and worked by day, hastening on to the completion of our task. At times, arriving at our destination in the middle of the night, we rested, exhausted, in the ladies' waiting-room at the railway station, where there were cane-seated settees, on which we spread our travelling rugs and remained until the morning. A native woman was always in charge, and good refreshment-rooms were at hand, so that we saved much time and avoided publicity in this way. We often travelled in what were known as "intermediate compartments," knowing that we should attract less attention than as first or second-class passengers. We simply asked for guidance at every step of the way through these months of anxiety and toil; and we knew that our prayers were answered.

We had various interpreters. One of these was a specially gifted woman. She had a sweet, plaintive voice, and sang the native songs with touching effect on the poor women whom we visited; one we always recall as having been a wonderful instrument through God of moving their hearts. It was a pilgrim hymn with a recurring strain of warning against the love of the world, dress, jewellery, and sinful pleasures; and reminding us all that this life is swiftly passing, and that death may soon overtake us. Often before the refrain was finished the poor women would be seen sobbing as they listened, joining in the sorrowful strain that recurred again and again; and as soon as the song was ended pouring out their pitiful histories and their protests against the degradation into which they had been thrust by the infamous system of legalised vice under which they were slaves.

II.

SEEKING THE OUTCAST.

A VIVID scene comes before us: We are sitting on a mortar bench, built in a circular form around the trunk of an old tree, in the open court of a Government chakla in one of the Cantonments of India. Some thirty or forty girls come trooping around us, either sitting down on the ground, native style, or bringing their cot-beds with them for seats.

Our sweet-voiced interpreter sings a plaintive song—native words and native tune—and when she has finished there is scarcely a dry eye to be seen. Then follows a simple Gospel message to which all give respectful heed, and at its close we ask, "Why are you in such a place as this?" Several answer in brief monosyllables, accompanied by a gesture as though drawing a line transversely across the brow. "It is our fate! It is our fate!" are the words used in reply; and our interpreter explains to us that these believe, in accordance with their religious instructions, that while they were yet babes, in an unfortunate moment, when left alone by the mother, the messenger of fate entered the room and wrote the word "prostitute" in invisible characters across the brow, and that from that moment to struggle against the lot that awaited them would have been useless.

No wonder that such poor slaves, when once taken and placed with the British soldiers by some wicked mahaldarni, never dream of trying to get away; and small wonder if others who had hoped that a better fate might await them, and who make one ignorant, feeble attempt to escape (and the women of a people whose customs keep them in perpetual seclusion are extremely ignorant of the outside world) and are recaptured by the police, will never be induced to try again, but quickly become convinced that their fate has been also inexorably fixed from the cradle.

"But," we say, "God is too good; He would not have it so." And they reply hopelessly, "But what can we do? We cannot starve; we cannot cut our own throats. Oh, that we might die!"

Then they begin to clamour for a chance to tell their individual stories. One is a girl who was left an orphan at the age of six years. At the tender age of eleven she says she was taken by an Englishman and kept three years as his mistress. When he deserted her, there was no door open to receive her but the chakla. One pretty girl said she had been deceived by a bad woman, under promise of employment.

Another, with face partly covered by her hands for very shame, said her husband had sold her to the mahaldarni for money. By graphic gesture and with the help of the few English words she knew, another told of the agonies of slow starvation until at last her courage gave way, and she came to the British soldiers, who were willing to feed her starving body for the sake of its worth as an instrument of self-indulgence. This is the only right to existence accorded to many women, even in so-called Christian countries, where labour is hard to obtain.

A little girl of ten, gaudily arrayed in the style of the others, thus publishing her candidature for a life of vice before she knew its meaning in the least, played about among the older ones. A little boy of two, with beautiful forehead, and other features that betrayed his English blood, had been forsaken by his father, who had, the girls said, "gone home to England." We recall having seen other children of Saxon type at Lucknow, Meerut, and at Peshawar, left in the same way by fathers who were officers of the British army in India. While the attempt is being made to create sentiment in favour of protecting the "innocent wives and children" of British soldiers, it might be well to inquire which wives and which children—those that already exist in India, or those that have not yet materialised in England. God knows which are the real wives and the real children of soldiers who have, in many cases in the past, entered into a contract with unsophisticated native women who never dreamed that it was anything less than lawful marriage!

"These bad women promise us everything and then betray us into this life," said several of the girls, referring to the treachery of the mahaldarnis. They told us of a girl who had recently been set on fire by an angry soldier, and had been burned to death, and related the story of cruelties practised upon them by drunken soldiers. A native guard in uniform drew near to listen. These military guards were there all the time, and were changed every few hours, the girls told us. As the mahaldarnis who own the girls are always at hand to watch against the escape of the discontented, the work of the guard seems to be chiefly to keep order and to prevent the entrance of native men, as the latter are strictly forbidden to associate with women kept for the English soldiers.

Two women of mature years now approached, and we were informed that they were the mahaldarnis. One lived there all the time, and the other was there with her girls for the time being. They said they had each a salary of ten rupees a month from the Government. They also took a share of the girls' earnings. Another time we went to the hut, close to the chakla, where one of them lived, and she proudly displayed to us some of the recommendations she held from British officers. They were grim and horrid reading; we will give but a single illustration:—

> "Ameer has supplied the 2nd Derby Regiment with prostitutes for the past three years, and I recommend her to any other regiment requiring her for a similar capacity.
>
> "S. G. M——,
>
> *"Quartermaster 2nd Derby Regiment."*

As to the methods to which these mahaldarnis resort to procure girls, it has been touched upon in the personal stories of girls already given, and will be emphasized necessarily more and more as our story continues. Mahaldarni Rahiman, met in another Cantonment, told us a story closely resembling the methods described in a former chapter (page 20), by a Government official. She said in substance: "If a girl is not sufficiently attractive to earn a living, I send her away and get another in her place. I get the women from the bazaar when more are needed. I go to the Cantonment magistrate, and he gives me five, ten, twenty, or fifty rupees, as the case may demand. To buy a very young, attractive girl I will be furnished with fifty rupees. There is always plenty of money to get them with."

When opportunity afforded, we called upon the other mahaldarni, and she likewise showed us her recommendations in the handwriting of British military officials, and other interesting papers which she had carefully preserved. There was an original copy of her appointment as mahaldarni to a certain regiment, closing with permission for her to go to Ferozepore to attend to "certain business of her bazaar." This was signed by the Colonel of the regiment. There was a letter written to her by the Staff-Surgeon of the same regiment, a few days later, saying:—

> "Mahaldarni, Seventh Lancers,—You have not brought your women from Meerut and Ferozepore. You will have to do it or the Colonel will think you have broken faith, as it is now fifteen days since you received your appointment."

The Staff-Surgeon evidently thought it an easy task to buy or entrap twelve or fifteen girls in as many days. Then there was a copy of a letter addressed by herself to the Cantonment magistrate, which she had employed some one to write in English for her. This letter stated that she had brought four new girls with her who had several thousand rupees' worth of jewelry with them (probably a lie by way of excuse), but their brothers had accompanied them (to effect their rescue?) and she asked the magistrate to require the girls to remain in the chakla, and then their brothers could not get near them. Native men not being allowed about the chakla, brothers and husbands who might be bent upon the rescue of female members of their families, who had been enticed away or stolen by the mahaldarnis, could be kept at a safe distance.

At other times we had opportunities to revisit this large chakla. There were about one hundred inmates, and accommodations for many more. The building was scarcely less than a huge fortification. High blank walls—excepting tiny well-barred windows high up, surrounded an open space of ground, or court; and the inner side of the wall was lined with small numbered rooms for the accommodation of the inmates. Most of the girls, here as elsewhere, because of constant association with British men, had learned to speak a little English, while a few spoke quite fluently. Although we always were accompanied by a good interpreter, yet often we were able to converse quite freely ourselves with the girls.

Our interpreter recognised one girl on our first visit, whom we shall call by her nickname, which was "Katy," and asked her if she was not the girl who had run after her carriage two or three times, begging the interpreter to take her away. Katy said she had done so, and with streaming tears reiterated her desire to escape from a life of which she was so ashamed, and pleaded with us to take her. When we consented to take her that very day, she faltered, and then decided that she did not dare try to go until after the following day, which was the day of the bi-weekly examination, but she said that if we would give her our address she would come herself on the day following. As we drove away in our cab, and the girls waved farewell, poor Katy, with pitiful and despairing countenance, burst into tears. Her face haunted us for days, and as she did not come of her own accord to us, in a few days we went after her again.

We learned afterwards that Katy had made ineffectual attempts to come to us. When we returned to the chakla for her, we found her without difficulty, and told her our errand. With glowing, happy face, she arrayed herself in her best garments, arranged her hair neatly and with childish simplicity, and leaving her few earthly belongings behind, got into the cab with us. But soon her face clouded, she grew apprehensive, and said she would have to go and get permission of the Cantonment magistrate before she could venture to leave. Anticipating not the slightest difficulty in this matter, when we represented the case to the magistrate and became surety for the girl's future good conduct and maintenance by a responsible Mission, we decided that it was best to let her have her own way. We did not then know India as we learned it afterwards. But the native policemen, seeing the girl with us, and being informed or suspecting our errand, refused, on enquiry, to inform us where the Cantonment magistrate could be found, and misled us in so far as they gave us any information.

We had a long, wearisome search, from which we learned somewhat of the difficulties that a poor Government slave-girl would encounter in trying, unaided, to disentangle herself from a life in the chakla. We took Katy away in the morning; we drove about, back and forth, mile upon mile, being sent hither and thither by misleading directions, and at last, considerably after mid-day, reached the magistrate's court, and entered. We were received with respect and given seats. In the course of our search, the girl had told us that her real fear of leaving without the magistrate's consent grew out of the fact that she had made one attempt to run away, and had been caught and fined, and had not yet paid the fine. She felt that if she went away again, without permission, it would only be to be ferreted out and fined yet more heavily. The timid girl, however, did not dare admit the whole truth to us, lest we might not consent to take her at all. Afterwards, we learned it from most reliable sources.

The girl had a very wicked mother and sister. An Englishman, who had known her from childhood, said that Katy had frequently come to him, saying she wished to be good and wanted to learn to read; but no way opened, apparently, for her to get free from the evil influences by which she was surrounded; and at last she was overcome, and became the "kept woman" of a British soldier at an early age. The soldier brought drink to their house, which she, in ignorance of the very strict laws to the contrary, permitted him to do. A native woman in the household of the man who related the facts to us, complained to the magistrate, and Katy was summoned to appear before him for punishment.

Frightened at the prospect, she managed to escape to a neighbouring village, was apprehended, brought back, sentenced to seven months' imprisonment, and a fine of fifty rupees for contempt of court. When she had served out her sentence (three months before we knew her) the mahaldarni was allowed (Katy said) to take her into custody and become surety for the fine. The English gentleman could not tell us whether the girl's statement that the mahaldarni was allowed to become her security was correct or not; but he believed it to be, from the fact that it was then that she went to the chakla and for the first time became a common prostitute. Learning these facts afterwards, we did not longer wonder that Katy had feared to try to come away without the magistrate's consent, and had shown such lack of courage when she faced him.

Almost immediately upon our seating ourselves in the court-room the poor girl burst into tears and ran outside and hid round a corner. It was with great difficulty that we persuaded her to come back and face the magistrate, who apparently was treating her with the utmost kindness. After considerable parleying in Hindustani and English, the magistrate at last acceded to our wishes, and wrote out a permit for us to take the girl away from the Cantonment, although he explained again and again that she or any other woman was of course free to go; they never attempted to detain a woman against her will, etc., etc. But Katy was not willing to proceed on any uncertainty, and she then asked about the fine, and was assured that would be all right.

The magistrate then explained that she had been arrested on "some criminal charge,"—he did not quite know what—had fled the Cantonment, been arrested and brought back and fined fifty rupees for contempt of court. He made no mention of her long imprisonment in addition. After that he began to set forth to her, in Hindustani (the meaning of his threats we did not fully understand), that if she went out of the Cantonment she would never be safe from the insults of soldiers, nor protected from molestation, nor allowed ever again to see her relatives, etc., etc., until her courage wavered, and she said, "Then I don't want to go." At this he thundered at her so angrily that once again she ran from the court-room, and it was with the utmost difficulty we persuaded her to go back for the final adjustment of the case. On her return she began to plead to be allowed to see her friends; and the magistrate, then turning to us, advised us in a kindly tone to take her to see her mother and sister before removing her entirely from them.

This the girl herself desired, so we felt obliged to accede, and she gave the cabman the address in Hindustani. Returning in the carriage, down an unfamiliar street, we alighted, and Katy ran ahead in all haste to find her mother, while we followed after. To our astonishment, we found we had entered the chakla again, from a side we had not recognised, and by an entrance which we had never before seen. We took alarm at once, and hastened on toward the wretched old woman who lay ill on a cot on the verandah, with whom Katy was talking earnestly.

A big, coarse woman (this was Katy's sister, but it must not be forgotten that we at this time did not know that her family were so disreputable) came out and sat down on the cot by the sick woman; but as soon as she heard enough of the girl's pleading to know that she was asking permission to escape from her wretched existence, she flew into a passion and struck Katy, and blow would have followed blow had we not interfered. Poor Katy flung herself dejectedly into a chair, and could not summon up courage to follow us against all this opposition; then a British soldier came up and spoke to her and led her away, while two or three more British soldiers looked on in contemptuous amusement at the scene. The poor creature was too cowed in spirit, from constant bad usage, to resist the determination of officials and soldiers to keep possession of so attractive a slave.

Weigh the soul of that one dark-skinned heathen girl against the diseased bodies of a standing army of men, and God knows which has most weight in his sight, even if a whole materialistic nation may have forgotten. Men and women, Governments and Armies, cannot, combined, reduce the estimate which He puts upon one immortal soul; but in a near judgment-day, these will have to drink the full measure appointed for such a crime as thwarting a woman in her God-given right to lead a decent moral life. When a Government begins to drag down the moral character of its subjects, it has begun to dig out its own foundations.

We talked with over three hundred Cantonment women, held to prostitution by the iron law of military regulation, collected together by Government procuresses, who were used as the ultimate tools of administration in carrying out Lord Roberts' military order for a sufficient number of attractive women, forced to the indecent exposure of their persons by misnamed "doctors," under penalty of fine or expulsion from the Cantonment, which was tantamount to starvation; imprisoned for several days of each month, even when in perfect health, in the Lock Hospital; imprisoned for an indefinite length of time in the hospital whenever found diseased; often turned out when seriously diseased, with their British children, to starve, or to spread disease at will among the natives, the final scapegoats of British profligacy; dismissed to starvation when too old to be any longer "sufficiently attractive" to the soldier, if only a fresh victim could be found to take the place; universally so poor as to be weighed down by debts, and receiving a pittance fixed by military usage, that kept many of them on the verge of starvation.

What were the circumstances that brought women to such a lot as this? We will give only a few, in bare outlines, of the many cases not already mentioned:—

1. A nurse-maid enticed to the chakla by a British sergeant.

2. A wife brought by her own husband, the man himself being engaged by an officer of the regiment as a servant, and allowed to hold his unwilling wife in such servitude.

3. British, granddaughter of a former Governor-General, daughter of a General, wife of a Commissioner; eloped with a soldier, and when deserted entrapped by a Mohammedan and kept as a slave, to whom British soldiers resorted in troops, almost, because a white woman; they paid the price of shame to her native master; rescued when almost dead. We found her in a miserably dirty bed at a native Lock Hospital, where the Government allowed her four annas (about fourpence) a day for subsistence. We ourselves rescued another British woman from the clutches of the same Mohammedan slave-holder. We found her in a fortified room, built on the top of a large house, a neck-breaking outside stairway leading to her abode. She had suffered horribly at the hands of the British soldiers admitted to her. Her reason was in-

jured beyond repair. In the absence of her master, she was guarded by a native servant armed with a knife, who had been instructed in her presence to plunge it into her if she tried to escape. A very courageous gentleman accompanied us, and succeeded in so frightening her master that we were permitted to lead her away.

4. An orphan seized by a wicked woman and reared to shame.

5. A young girl brought by her own brother and sold to the chakla.

6. Cabul girl of high birth who lost her father in the Afghan war. She was only twelve when left without protection, and her father's groom persuaded her to come away with him under promise of marriage; sold by him to shame. She wept bitterly, exclaiming, "Oh, the shame of being pointed out as a bazaar woman!" We asked her why she did not go to the Cantonment magistrate and plead her own case, for she said she had money secreted with which she could take care of herself, if once she could get away. She replied, "Why should I tell him? I am only a black woman; I fear him." When about to return to the south, we revisited this station and hunted this woman up, offering to assist her to escape; but her courage failed at the last moment, and we were obliged to leave her behind to her fate.

7. An Egyptian woman from Cairo, enticed away from her home when a child and sold to an old woman in Quetta, then carried to India.

8. A Kashmiri woman; ill-treated by her husband, she ran away with another man who promised to make her his wife, but sold her into shame. "It is a bad job; I don't like it," she said in the best English she could control, while the tears were in her eyes.

9. A hill girl of respectable family lost her parents and her husband (perhaps only betrothed, yet possibly already married), before ten years of age. A deceitful woman came to comfort her in her grief and unprotected condition, and enticed her to travel with her a month to assuage her grief; sold her to a British official, with whom she lived one year, when he died. She then became a chakla woman. She was only sixteen. She said, "It is a bitter life."

10. A high-caste Brahmin girl, not able to understand a word of the language of her captor, found deserted and starving. The captor admitted that she was a perfectly respectable girl, yet she was examined by the surgeon, her name entered on the list of prostitutes, and taken to the Lock Hospital to be prepared for her fate. The poor thing was so grateful to be taken in and fed, and little dreamt of what would be demanded of her in return. We tried in vain to make her understand us, and to warn her of her fate.

11. Taken in famine time by the daughter of a sepoy (native soldier). The soldier sold her at eleven years of age "to sit in the chakla." "In all the years of my life, I have not known one day of happiness; my heart is full of wounds," was her pathetic ending of the story.

12. We witnessed the purchase of a girl by a mahaldarni. A woman seized the girl as payment for a debt, and bringing her sold her to the mahaldarni in our very presence.

13. Married at eleven, and widowed almost immediately. After three years with her family as a widow, she was so miserable that she ran away and wandered in the streets. She was arrested by the police, and at the age of fourteen put in the chakla.

14. Her husband was beating her cruelly, at the age of fourteen, and she ran away; a policeman seized her and sent her to the Lock Hospital.

15. Deserted at the age of eleven by her husband; a British man took her by force to his bungalow. When he discarded her, her family would not receive her again. She was then "taken by the Government and put in the chakla."

III.

THE HABITATIONS OF CRUELTY.

IN March, 1892, we arrived at a huge Cantonment about midnight. As there was no dak bungalow at the place, we spread our rugs on the settees in the ladies' waiting-room, and slept till morning. The dak bungalow is an institution kept up by the Government for the convenience of military men and their families, although other travellers take advantage of its shelter, and was preferable to an hotel for our purpose, for our meals were served in our private rooms always, and we could lead a very retired life. After breakfast in the dining-room, we went out and engaged a cab, explaining, as was our custom, to the driver, that we were Christian missionaries, and in accordance with the teachings of our religion, we were searching out the most despised and disreputable of women, to tell them of God's care for them and to see what we could do for them; therefore we wished him to drive us to see the chakla women of the Cantonment. He looked a little bewildered, and then drove off with us.

After traversing a considerable distance, he entered a public garden, and began to drive slowly, that we might enjoy the flowers and foliage. We called to him, bidding him drive on rapidly, as we did not care to see the sights of the Cantonment. He nodded assent, and touching his horse with the whip, drove away in another direction. Presently he paused before another object to which he was accustomed to take visitors. Then we called him from his seat to the cab window, and told him that if he took us out of our way again, we should be obliged to leave his cab, call another, and dismiss him. We made sure he understood exactly what we wished, and he admitted that he did, but intimated that he scarcely thought it a proper place for us to visit. However, he consented, and drove off, and in a few moments brought us to an open field where two regiments were encamped. Fortunately, some drill of an unusual sort was going on, and a good many people had driven out to witness it; this, therefore, absorbed the attention of all. The Lord appointed all our seasons for us during our Indian investigations.

Taking a road leading to the back part of the camp, we left our cab and driver where several other cabs were standing, and walking along together, observed by no one, entered one of the ten little tents we found enclosed in a sort of fence of matting. The women received us cordially, although with real astonishment at such unusual visitors. The mahaldarni was not a bad-meaning woman in many regards, and she told us, with great satisfaction, of a sister of hers who had been promoted from the rank of a common soldiers' woman to be a mahaldarni, saying that she had left off her wickedness, prayed four times a day and read her Koran.

She joined with her girls in expressions of utter abhorrence of the examinations to which the girls were subjected, saying, "Shame! Shame!"

She told us how the soldiers, when in drink, knocked the poor girls about in a most cruel manner, and reaching her own conclusion as to the meaning of our call, advised us not to join their number, telling us that the city was far preferable. She and the girls told of the heavy fines to which they would be liable if they did not go to the examinations, or attempted to leave the Lock Hospital when held there. She said if they made any fuss about the fine, then they would be imprisoned. A military guard was placed within the enclosure, in one of the tents; but he had either gone to sleep, or wandered out to get a view of the exercises that were going on near by. We gave a simple gospel talk through our interpreter, and she sang and prayed with the girls; then we made our way to the women of the adjoining Rest Camp.

Again we entered the enclosure surrounding the little tents, and reached the women without attracting the attention of the guard. They told the same story of compulsion and fines continually hanging over their heads. Almost every Cantonment girl we ever questioned, was held to her wretched life by debt and fines, so that she could not think of getting free without being apprehended on account of them. Here likewise they warned us not to join them, but go rather to the city. Again we talked of Jesus, the Friend of the oppressed, and after song and prayer, bade them good-bye.

Returning to our cab, we told our driver to take us to the Lock Hospital; and after a long drive under the burning sun, we stopped before buildings enclosed within a very high brick wall with broken glass on its top to prevent the escape of inmates. A large, strongly-spiked gateway, with double doors, gave the impression of a veritable prison; and there, standing in the open gateway, was an uniformed armed guard. Previous experiences had not led us to expect anything quite so formidable, although there was generally some sort of a guard or watchman at hand, and the native physician usually resided on the premises. We had often said, and promised God, that, sacred as was the nature of the work, we would never prevaricate in order to cover up our real object, if closely questioned. We were not ordinary detectives, playing a part, but Christian women, and the difference was not to be lost sight of.

Our interpreter had not been instructed as to the full significance of our work, but was content to ask few questions if only she might be allowed to follow her bent freely and preach the gospel, which we gladly encouraged and helped in every way possible, for we should have felt that our mission was very incomplete had we met these women solely to hear their pitiful stories, and never utter a word to them of the love of the Heavenly Father, in the midst of such distressing surroundings. Our interpreter always carried religious tracts with her; and while we were hesitating to know how to encounter the armed sentinel, in the simplicity of her holy zeal she walked up to him, gave him a tract, and said a few words of a helpful nature. The guard noticed no more than that some ladies were being delayed at the gate, so he motioned us through, continuing his consideration of the leaflet, and forgetting to ask our errand. How easy for God to hide his own as He had hidden us again and again that day from guard and sentinel! We have frequently been asked how we escaped observation. We can only say that we made but little effort on our own part to do this, and trusted the Lord to do it all for us.

A dozen women gathered around us in a ward of the hospital that day. With them we had a little service, as usual, after which they eagerly poured out their sad life stories, and told of the oppressions of the system under which they were held in an evil life. The hospital nurse showed us through the wards and the examination room, where we found the grim rack for the torture of the examination, brutal to the patient, but convenient for the surgeon to do as much villainy as possible in a given length of time. No diseases are so rife or dreadful in their consequences but that their compulsory treatment, when it involves the indecent exposure of woman or man, is worse in its effects than the disease itself. And this in the case of actual disease. What, then, can be said as an excuse for such exposure simply to find out whether there be disease? Yes, further, what possible plea can be made when the object of such compulsory exposure is to discover whether the subject is "fit"[4] for a life of infamy?

Mrs. Butler has well expressed the encouragement to vice that the compulsory examination of women leads to in the following words: "We all approve of healing disease and taking care of the sick, no matter what has brought on their disease, no matter how sinful and degraded they may be. The Abolitionists have always pleaded for plenty of free hospital accommodation for men and women afflicted with this curse. But it will be clear to you that this law is not for simple healing, as Christ would have us heal, caring for all, whatever their character, and whatever their disease. This law is invented to provide beforehand, that men may be able to sin without bodily injury—if that were possible, which it is not. If a burglar, who had broken into my house and stolen my goods, were to fall and be hurt, I would be glad to get him into a hospital and have him nursed and cured; but I would not put a ladder up against my window at night and leave the windows open, in order that he might steal my goods without danger of breaking his neck."

But to return to the Lock Hospital mentioned. The nurse produced the records for our examination. In the correspondence book was the copy of a letter from the military surgeon, informing the Cantonment magistrate of six girls suspected of disease, and asking that they be apprehended and sent to the hospital for examination. That looked simple enough, and why not?

Imagine yourself the one apprehended, and the case assumes a different aspect. A policeman comes to your door and reads a warrant for your arrest as a common prostitute; you ask on what authority; you are informed that the name of the informant is not made public, because if a man can be induced to help trace out diseases—it being regarded as a "point of honour" to inform other men where danger lurks—his confession must not be made known, it would injure his reputation. (We are now describing the exact conditions always existent where there is compulsory examination of women.)

You contend that you have a right to your good name, and that it is a principle

[4] An official form of expression.

of justice that no one can be punished on secret and unproved evidence, and that it is punishment of the worst sort to be taken by a policeman through the streets to a hospital used exclusively for the treatment of a certain class of disorders. You are then informed that unless you will go at once without any trouble, you will be taken out of the town in which you live, set down as a common vagrant by the roadside, and if ever again found within the limits of the city in which your parents, brothers, and sisters live, you will be arrested and put in jail. What will you do? Yet these were exactly the laws under which these poor women, among whom we were spending the day, lived.

By such a system of delivering over the bodies of women as public property, any woman of humble circumstances upon whom any man of lecherous design casts his eyes, could be made to come to his terms of existence by the aid of the police force, if necessary, and magistrates of evil design could condemn any woman to a life of prostitution. And in this hospital all this wicked compulsion was set down in a book, every page of which was headed, "Prostitutes attending Voluntary Inspections."

From the Lock Hospital we drove to a large chakla, and talked with a group of about twenty girls, among them a little girl of twelve, and another of four. Everywhere we went among the degraded women of India, we found children in the chaklas, these Government-regulated brothels, with their ever-present guards, so that Englishmen knew perfectly that children were being trained under Government regulation for prostitution. The advocates of licensed prostitution for India are fond of insisting as an excuse for licensing the evil, that it does no great harm because the recruits come from "the prostitute caste." Repeatedly we made enquiries of Englishmen, native physicians, and in one case applied to the census office for some information concerning this special class. Its existence was practically denied, excepting those cases which can be found in every land, in which women of all classes may fall into shame and train their daughters after their own evil ways. It is scarcely necessary in this connection to mention the temple and nautch girls of India, who are found in civil lines. They are a wholly distinct class from the enslaved women who are set apart to minister to the vices of the British soldiers. Among the latter we found Hindus of all castes, from high-caste Brahmins down; and we also found Mohammedans, Arabs, Egyptians, Afghans, Kashmiris, Jewesses,—recruits, in fact, from those among whom "caste" does not prevail. If it were true that all these chakla women constitute one caste, for what object did the Government of India, in times past, provide invariably (so far as our observation extends) for a record of the "caste" of the women to whom registration tickets were given? The ticket which we purchased of a woman at Meean Meer in 1892 (a fac-simile of which is given in this volume, *Appendix B*) recorded her "name," "caste," "registered number," "place of residence," "date of registry," and "personal appearance."[5]

But there is a class in India being trained to prostitution, though not a "caste," properly speaking, and they are getting their training in the brothels established

[5] For forms of tickets of registration of prostitutes see Departmental Committee Report (1893), pages 12, 331, 334, and 335.

and managed by Englishmen, and many of the candidates in this class are the children of Englishmen, who have been deliberately placed there, or allowed to go there, by their inhuman fathers. This is, properly speaking, the prostitute class of India, those born to their fate; the reader may judge whether the existence of the class justifies licensing it for the purpose.

In the chakla we sang, "Where He leads me I will follow," and its interpretation constituted our Gospel message. With tears in their eyes the girls assured us, with characteristic gesture, that we were "on their eyes and on their hearts"; in other words, had won their affections; and spoke feelingly of the honour it was to them that Englishwomen should come to see them, saying that usually Englishmen forbade their wives to even look at them. One girl said that when at Cawnpore missionaries used to come to them, and that for days after their visits her heart was so sore that it seemed as if it would burst. The girls stood in the doorway, many of them with streaming eyes, and waved good-bye as we departed, begging us to come again soon.

We hastened to the railway station for the three o'clock train. When we alighted, we spoke a few kind words to our cabman, for he had served us most faithfully, all these hours under the mid-day glare of the sun, after so unpromising a beginning. We wished to pay him well, and asked him to set his own price on his services. The simple, rough native man hesitated a moment, stammered something unintelligible, burst into tears, and averting his face with noble shame, said, "I don't want anything at all. I never saw anything like this before; I would like to help, too." Thrusting a coin into his unwilling hand, ample for both fee and present, we hastened to our seats in the car, and were soon rolling away to our next destination. We wrote up our notes of the day's doings on the way, and arrived at our next field of operations the following morning at two o'clock, stealing into another Cantonment unobserved, excepting by the Heavenly Father, without whom not even a sparrow can fall. We give this history of one day as a sample; the work was heavy and painful; but we encouraged each other often with the words, "Even if we fall by the way, we could not die in better work."

We visited a Rest Camp at Meerut. As usual, we had no difficulty in passing the sentinels; God took care of that. We learnt from official records that the regiment had only been in India two weeks; yet the complete paraphernalia of vice was at hand. There were fourteen little tents for women, and near their quarters a huge tent pitched for those who wished to smoke opium. Think of it, fathers and mothers, boys of the age of from eighteen years upwards, supplied by their superior officers, before they could have made a demand for the same, with every convenience for giving themselves over to debauchery! The sight of their fresh young faces touched us deeply.

At another place, away up on the northern frontier, we found only five girls; the others had somehow escaped their cruel bondage. As we entered the gateway of the mud wall that surrounded their quarters, a native man standing near threw up his hands in great astonishment, exclaiming, "O God! ('Allah'), how wonderful that ladies should come to such a place!" It was a dreary, weird scene. The evening was piercingly cold, and we were well wrapped. The old mahaldarni and her girls were trying to warm themselves by a wretched little pot of charcoal, stretching their thin fingers by turns over the coals.

While we talked, the sudden night of a country without a twilight came on, although it was not really very late. One of the girls lighted a native lamp of the rudest sort—a bit of wick floating in an earthenware cup of oil—and set it in a niche in the wall. The room was unfurnished excepting the *charpoy*, or cot bed, on which we sat. The girls and mahaldarni sat, native fashion, on the floor, their cotton chuddars and skirts fluttering in the cruel wind that came in at the open archway, for door there was none.

They said the men of their regiment were very bad, and often when drunk beat them and robbed them, not only refusing to pay them any money, but even taking away their cotton quilts and selling them to their own native servants for a few pice with which to buy drink. They described the case of one woman who was beaten terribly by a soldier, and cut in the arms and breast; after this, several of the girls had effected their escape. We have often spoken of this as one of the most deeply shaded pictures in our memory, not only because of the dreary, comfortless surroundings, but because of the cruelty and oppression that weighed these helpless women down, from which there seemed no hope of escape. We talked to them out of the fullness of our sympathy, and promised to pray and work in their behalf, that they, and others like them, might have an opportunity to turn to a good life.

But turning from the physical injury inflicted on these poor women, we wish to present a view of their mental sufferings. It has been urged by many advocates of the regulation of vice that the whole nature of a woman was changed by her sinful life—that she had no sensitiveness and no deep sense of the degradation of her position. We utterly deny this on behalf of the scores of women with whom we have talked in India—whether of high or of low caste, Hindoo or Mohammedan, and of whatever nationality; whether brought up in virtue and afterwards betrayed, or brought up from infancy in vicious surroundings. We deny it even in regard to the mahaldarnis placed over the women, whom avarice might blind, and the ordinary routine duties of their position might harden. Yet when their womanly feelings were appealed to, they always responded, and felt shame with and for the women under their care.

In all our conversations there was shown a most remarkable patience, on the part of the women, in regard to the various inconveniences and hardships which the regulations entailed upon them. The fire of their hatred and indignation all centred upon *the heart of the regulations, the examinations,* and the violation of womanhood which these examinations were felt to be. It is of no use for any one to deny to us that these women have deep feelings in regard to their wrongs and their shame. We have felt the beating of their aching hearts against our own; we have heard histories that throbbed with the strong agony of betrayed innocence; we have seen a hopeless woe in eyes that will haunt us for ever.

At Peshawar, the women said, when speaking of the great hardship of being turned out of the Cantonment, "Where can we go to? We are prostitutes. No one would give us work." And again, "Every one under this Government is treated well but ourselves; *we only are despised.*"

We do not present these facts with any thought of taking our position with those who argue that the better regulation of vice implies a better protection of the degraded women; but rather to show that in the working out of such regulations the *woman* is absolutely lost sight of, and only the *prostitute* is considered. Every interest in the woman's character, happiness, health, life itself, is made subservient to the health and convenience of the British soldier. Every assertion that would put a humanitarian gloss on the regulation of vice is utter hypocrisy.

At Meerut, where there were a good many women present, one, without any question whatever on our part, suddenly broke forth into the most intense expressions of disgust at the Governmental regulation of vice, in which those girls gathered about her sympathized, one especially taking part in the conversation from time to time, and corroborating what was being said. She said, "The Queen does not approve of this; it is the Commander-in-Chief and the officers who are doing these things! Oh, what a shame that the Government does these things!" Then she burst into a passion of indignation, describing in vivid language and with a natural eloquence of gesture the whole shameful proceeding, and the humiliation to which they were subjected.

Words fail to convey the force, and fire, and pathos with which that poor, untaught woman pleaded the cause of her sisters. It was one voice out of many protesting against this cruel wrong, and representing the undying dignity of a woman's nature, even when forced into a deeper abyss than she ever voluntarily chose to enter. We asked if the other women felt as this one did, and they all answered indignantly, "We all hate it." The first woman cried out, "It is very disgusting; oh, *shame*!" We told them it was a grief to us that those who called themselves Christians should do such things, and that they ought not to bear the name. She replied bitterly, "Yes; the Commander-in-Chief, the Colonel, and all of them, all the way down—your Christian men!—they all favour these things. The Queen does not countenance it, for she has daughters of her own; and she cares for her daughters in India also. It is the Commander-in-Chief" (meaning Lord Roberts).

The accounts we have given in previous pages reveal the extremely tender age at which some of these girls were thrust into a life of shame by court proceedings under the Contagious Diseases Acts, when they were openly enforced. Two Benares girls declared they were taken up by the police at fourteen, and one Sitapur girl said she was sold to a mahaldarni at eleven. Much has been said of the horrors of child-marriage in India, and these atrocities should not be minimized, even though we bear in mind the usually slender type of Eastern manhood; but what shall we say when the robust British soldier has had placed at his mercy a little girl of fourteen years old, of the delicate Oriental type; and this done by regular process of law "*to preserve his health*"?

Then again considering the heathen training of these women, we were led to expect that we should find blindness of the moral sense in relation to this sort of wrong-doing. On the contrary, they expressed great shame and humiliation, never tried to justify their sinful acts, spoke almost universally of their hatred of the life, shed bitter tears, and told us how burdened their hearts were in thinking of their sins. Unlike what we met elsewhere in speaking of religion to the natives, they had little desire for controversy. With not a single exception, we were made welcome, treated courteously, and listened to and blessed for our message. Even in the case of the mahaldarnis we found them not inaccessible, but inclined to expressions of contempt for the whole system of regulation, and of apology for being the hirelings of such a system—an excuse which must have more weight than in a country where industries are open to women. Rahiman of Meerut was an exception. She said she considered her business perfectly legitimate, because she was in a "Government position."

Several times we asked the women, "What do you wish us to do for you?" and were surprised at the answer. Desperately poor as many were, there was never an appeal for money; rather they said, "Pray for us;" or, "If you would build us homes, so that we could go to them, and not sin any more, what more could we ask?" and, "If you will help us to have the examinations stopped." Above all, we were astonished at the appeals made to us concerning the latter outrage. We told none of them our whole object in coming among them, yet with great care they described and expressed their abhorrence of the examinations, as well as the wickedness and illegality of them; and in two or three instances they mentioned that they had heard of ladies interested in their behalf, and suggested the possibility that we might do something for them. In one instance several of the women, after telling us of their humiliation, clasped their hands together, and lifting their eyes to heaven, prayed to God that He would "help us to help them." They invariably exonerated the Queen from all blame in this matter, saying, "She is a woman herself; she would not do this. She cares for her daughters in India."

Says Mrs. Josephine Butler: "It is impossible not to think of the fathers and mothers of the young Englishmen, mere boys, who go out to India as soldiers, and who are trained in this disgusting manner by the military authorities; not only in the indulgence of their vices, but in cowardly and brutal cruelties towards the weaker sex. It seemed a grand object indeed on the part of Lord Roberts and his subordinates to aim at sending back their discharged soldiers to England free from physical disease, regardless of their manliness, their moral character, their respect for women, and decent habits of life! Would not the loss of these be bought too dearly by the mere exemption from physical disease, even if this could be made possible?"

After months of toil, we were now far up towards the north-western frontier of India. We requested our cabman to drive us to the quarters of the Government women of the Cantonment. We left the cab just outside the narrow street. As we walked past the native shops and turned into a little sort of lane, a woman shouted in great concern from her doorway to us, "Why do you come here? Don't come here; all are prostitutes who live here." With a smile of re-assurance we replied, "We know it, and you are just the women we are seeking; we have a message for you."

With surprise, she then welcomed us most warmly and invited us in, saying she would go and call all the women and bring them to hear the message. In a few minutes chairs had been borrowed for us to sit upon, and nine native women were clustered on the floor at our feet.

We both exclaimed regarding the remarkable personal appearance of the woman who had addressed us first. She closely resembled, in fine bearing and apparent intellectuality, a much-beloved mutual friend in Chicago, a woman of more than local fame in scientific pursuits; it touched us deeply. With utmost simplicity and confidence this woman came and seated herself by Mrs. Andrew's side, leaning her arm across her lap, and many a time during the interview that followed, her earnest, wistful eyes met ours, while Mrs. Andrew gently stroked her shoulder, her heart almost breaking with pity as the woman told her sad story.

A plaintive native song was sung by our interpreter, and tears flowed freely. After that the simple Gospel message was given. They told us then some of the painful details of the conditions under which they were living, saying that they must either meet these conditions or be expelled from the Cantonment, and added, "If we are expelled, where shall we go? we must leave all our friends, and no one will give us work. It means great hardship; we would starve." Speaking of the hateful examinations, they said the Queen had forbidden these things, but the officers yet compelled them to go on.

The woman at Mrs. Andrew's side told us the following: "Some time ago a lady in Calcutta saw a woman weeping as she was going to the Lock Hospital with other women. The lady asked her why she wept. She told why she was obliged to go, and how she hated the examinations.

"The lady could not understand this, but took the woman home with her, and closely questioned into the matter. Then the lady said to her, 'This ought not to be,' and promised that she would do all she could for them. Then the lady went home to England and talked to the Queen. She spoke with wonderful power in behalf of the poor women of India. She said to the Queen that she (the Queen) was a woman, and these in India were women, and their shame was the Queen's shame, and for them to be outraged was as though she (the Queen) was outraged, that it was a shame for *women* to be treated so when a woman was Queen. Then the Queen ordered it to be stopped. But the officers still carry it on." This she added sorrowfully, all the other women joining in the assertion. Then a sudden thought came into the woman's face, and she asked: "Are you like that lady of Calcutta, going to try to do something to help us?" We told them we would work and pray for them that help might come and homes be provided for them. They blessed and thanked us over and over. We told them, "We are your sisters;" they replied, *"We are your slaves."*

Then the woman whom we have especially described lifted her hand and with impressive solemnity uttered a vow that she would no longer lead a life of shame.

The next morning we went back to the same place and stopped before the open door. The old mother was sitting on the floor by a little charcoal fire preparing the breakfast. The two daughters of the house were putting their simple little abode in order for the day. The penitent one came forward and smiled so faint a welcome, and seemed so embarrassed at our coming, that we at first thought she was offended; but they exclaimed almost instantly, "We were awake at midnight last night talking of you, and we said it must have been the true God who had sent you to tell us of your religion." We replied that they had been sorely on our hearts, so that we could not sleep, and that we too were awake at midnight, talking of them and praying for them. They then poured out blessings upon us, with hands clasped in prayer.

As we talked earnestly and lovingly to them, through our interpreter, the one who had made the solemn vow came forward and knelt beside Mrs. Andrew, who was standing, and timidly took her hand. Mrs. Andrew laid it on the poor girl's shoulder as on the day before, but the interpreter said, "Put your hand on her head; she is asking you to bless her." Tears streamed from the eyes of the penitent, and she shook with sobs as Mrs. Andrew fervently blessed her in the name of our God, and pleaded with Him for the way to open for her escape from bondage. Then in like manner the other daughter came and was blessed. Then the poor old mother threw herself with her forehead on the ground, laying her hands on Mrs. Andrew's feet, and while Mrs. Andrew prayed over her, groaned and cried bitterly, saying, "I am a sinner, I am a sinner. For twenty-five years I led a life of shame, and brought up my daughters to it."

We then wrote down their names, promising to pray for them, a pledge which we have faithfully kept ever since.

IV.

THE CONTAGIOUS DISEASES ACTS.

THE advocates of State-regulated fornication contend that diseases due to vice will be best checked by licensed prostitution, combined with medical care. The Abolitionists hold that morality alone is sufficient, and that vice is not necessary. It is a square issue; shall it be immorality and medicine, or shall it be morality?

The Regulationists believe that vice is necessary; the Abolitionists believe that vice is not necessary, and that virtue must be demanded. A memorial signed by one hundred and twenty-three British women, of whom over half belong to the titled aristocracy, presented to the British Government April 24, 1897, declares:—

"We feel it is the duty of the State, which of necessity, collects together large numbers of unmarried men in military service, to protect them from the consequences of evils which are, in fact, unavoidable."

A memorial, on the other hand, of sixty-one thousand four hundred and thirty-seven British women, and presented to the Government July 31, 1897, asserts:—

"No permanent diminution of disease will ever be attained by measures which do not strike primarily at the vice itself."

The leader of the sixty-one thousand and more, Mrs. Josephine Butler, answers to the statement of the one hundred and twenty-three: "The confidence of ultimate victory based on a foundation which cannot be shaken, enables us to regard with composure the forward advance and claims of materialism and fleshly indulgence, and to compassionate those—furious against us to-day—who will be beaten to-morrow, and who will be forced, before the 'great cloud of witnesses' in heaven and earth, to confess themselves defeated and deserving of defeat."

The cause of venereal disease is promiscuous relations carried to excess. The hope of eradicating such disease, then, by licensing its cause, betokens the extreme of moral blindness, and contradicts all science. Dr. Elizabeth Blackwell says: "We may as well expect to cure typhoid fever whilst allowing sewer gas to permeate the house; or cholera, whilst bad drinking water is being taken, as try to cure venereal disease whilst its cause remains unchecked."

A recent official plea for licensed prostitution in the Cantonments of India declares: "The efforts to teach the soldiers habits of self-control" have "signally failed." We wish for a moment to consider the efforts that have been used in the past. There lies before us a copy of the "Report of the Army Health Association." It was printed at Meerut, India, in 1892. We have also the subsequent reports for several years. In speaking of the efforts put forth to teach self-control, much is made of the work of this Association (see Departmental Committee Report, 1897, page 13), as a means that has been used. This report of the Army Health Association has printed on its cover such texts as, "Keep thyself pure," "He that soweth to his flesh shall of the flesh reap corruption," etc.; giving the impression that it is a religious document. In fact it is interspersed all through with Scripture quotations.

The introduction is signed by a Major-General, and the body of the report is written by an army chaplain, secretary to the Association, who has the title of Bachelor of Divinity. Four reverends beside, army chaplains, are named among the list of officers of the Association. The language employed in the report is often very obscure, and needs close analysis to get at its real meaning. The introduction is a plea for the re-establishment of the abolished system of Regulation, and is little more than the expression of a desire to have legal sanction for what they were already doing illegally, as the report shows, and it is doubtless for this very reason that the language is so obscure. In one place it speaks of the "Gospel duty of healing diseases in a compulsory way," and as a precedent refers to the "Gospel record of healing even when a voice had come from the healed protesting against the cure." Certainly blasphemy could scarcely go further than to liken the compulsory indecent exposure of a woman to a miracle of our Lord. Every soldier should "do his best," says the report, "by the blessing of Almighty God, to resist all temptation leading to the evil." Close inspection proves that in this case "the evil" in the mind of the writer is not the vice but the disease. The soldier is recommended to the task of attaining to "self-command on pass," *i.e.*, when outside the region of licensed brothels.

The report states that a "Handbook" has been circulated "to all fresh arrivals in India," and the closing chapter of the report is a reprint of that Handbook, which is especially designed for army chaplains to circulate among the soldiers as a "religious" tract. Interspersed with the quotations of Scripture texts, is abominable instruction to the effect that a young man who will confine his visits to the Government licensed brothel can trust the Lord to keep him from contracting disease. This "religious" tract promises to keep infected women out of the chakla, and warns the soldier not to go "in an underhand way" to houses where he will not be protected from "disease."

O mothers! can you conceive of what would be your feeling to discover that your eighteen-year-old boy, as is the son of many an English mother, was under such "gospel" instruction as this! "We shall never forget what we owe to Lord Roberts," says the report; and we might have anticipated that the author of the "Infamous Memorandum" would likewise be the supporter of such measures for the instruction of young soldiers. Sir George White, who succeeded Lord Roberts as Commander of the Indian forces, said, in the Viceregal Council held in India, July 8, 1897, that "Every effort should also be made to warn young soldiers of the consequences of immorality in this country, to point out to them the terrible risks which they run, and to appeal to their higher moral instincts and to their pride in their manhood to avoid connections that carry with them grave danger that they will return home shattered wrecks, unfit alike for military duty or civil life."

There is not one word here as though evil connections were likewise to be avoided, even if they were not supposed to carry danger of physical disease as a result. The "moral" teaching seems to have been all of that immoral sort that points toward the Government house of shame rather than to the seventh commandment. How many young soldiers may not have met their first temptation by having a superior officer point them to the Government-regulated chakla! Dr. Elizabeth Blackwell says truly: "The first indispensable condition in the prevention of disease is the steady discouragement of promiscuous intercourse. Now I assert positively that such discouragement has never been seriously tried in the army, by Government, but only by unofficial efforts—efforts which are most valuable, but entirely lacking in the force of organization, and in the important recognition and help which Government alone can afford."

It is easy to *assume* that the compulsory periodical examination of women will check diseases due to vice; but the assumption has never been proved. The statistics of the years during which the C. D. Acts prevailed in certain military stations in Great Britain, as compared with the statistics of later years, show a marked decrease since repeal took place, and therefore that the compulsory examinations in no way diminished disease, but rather the contrary. And when an unbiased person thoroughly investigates the history of the controversy on the subject, and is made acquainted with the course of deceit which has been practised in the past by Anglo-Indian[6] advocates of licensed vice, in order to maintain an odious system, a belief in Indian military assertions will not be inspired. The statement is being heralded to the world that over half the British army in India is suffering from diseases due to vice. Yet Lord George Hamilton, Secretary of State for India, was obliged to explain in the House of Commons, January 25, 1897, that while it had been reported that the aggregate of admissions to hospital for venereal diseases among the British troops in India amounted in 1895 to 522 per thousand, "This does not mean that 522 men per thousand were separately and individually admitted, still less does it indicate that 522 soldiers per thousand are incapacitated for duty from this cause. It is calculated on the latest returns that an average permanent reduction of 46 per thousand is the loss entailed by these diseases." In other words, instead of over half being incapacitated from military duty, less than one in twenty is off duty from this cause mentioned. The larger number, which is calculated to startle the public into submission to the demands of certain Anglo-Indian officials, has been secured on the assumption that every "admission" into hospital means a fresh case, whereas it has been conceded that all re-admissions from relapse, and every stage of the progress of disease which requires a new diagnosis, has been reckoned as an "admission." A Member of Parliament who has been enquiring about the hospital records, says:

> "I have before me the hospital sheet of a man who was in hospital from January 1st to January 25th in one year. During that time the medical description of his disease was changed four times, and the man is formally entered and discharged and re-admitted on each of these occasions, the date of each discharge and

[6] A term applied to British residents in India.

> admission being entered in the column provided for the purpose. So that this one man, who has been only once in hospital during the year, actually furnishes four 'admissions' to the official record. The same man was again in hospital from the 1st to the 30th of May, in the following year, during which time the diagnosis being three times changed, he was entered as admitted and discharged three times."

Statistics compiled on this basis are absolutely worthless for the purposes of argument, and indicate, when so used, a lack of conscience as to exact truthfulness. The official figures of the Indian Army (included in the Report of the Departmental Committee of 1897, strongly advocating a return to licensed prostitution), lie before us. It cannot be said that such a report would be likely to minimize the amount of disease, yet this report, on page 9, distinctly states: "In 1895 an average of 45 men per thousand, or 3,200 in a force of 71,031 British soldiers in India, were constantly in hospital for venereal diseases." Certainly this is sufficiently conclusive. The statement is heralded to the world that all England is becoming infected from the troops of diseased soldiers who return yearly to the home-land. One advocate of licensed prostitution in India says that "thirteen per cent." of the British soldiers are "annually invalided home, hopelessly incurable for military purposes." But referring to the same official statistics, embodied in the Departmental Committee's Report, we find that from the year 1887 to the year 1895, 681 men out of the force of 70,000 and more, were invalided home from these diseases, or, on an average, 76 men annually out of the whole force of 70,000; that is, *one-ninth of one per cent.* Such unworthy attempts to frighten an unwilling Christian public into acceding to the return to a system of licensed prostitution, cannot be too strongly condemned. Many well-meaning persons, on the assumption that "figures will not lie," are repeating these exaggerated assertions, and will not take the trouble of investigating for themselves. The Army Sanitary Commission testified in 1894 that "a compulsory Lock Hospital system in India has proved a failure." There could be no higher authority to quote; and the attempt to check diseases of this sort by the compulsory Lock Hospital system had then been carried on for the good part of a century in India. If the case could not be proved by such a prolonged experiment, involving such injustice to women, surely all honest people should be ready to favour its abandonment.

But it is proposed now in certain quarters to examine men as well as women. Two wrongs do not make a right. Equality of degradation is not the sort of equality for Christians to desire. Bring the test home. Could the reader, without committing sin, go to a physician to be examined in order to discover whether he or she is "fit" to practise fornication? Then the State that requires such an act becomes guilty in the sight of God of committing the act. The guilt of that which is done under actual compulsion rests wholly upon the State or individual that thus enforces wrong-doing. The one who advocates the compulsory examination of women stands guilty before God as the perpetrator of the outrage. It is a fearful thing when the State becomes the perpetrator of such sin. We know it is argued that the women and men subjected to such regulations would be only those who are willing to submit. We will dwell on that point a little further on; at present it is enough to say, that because a thief is willing to steal, the State is no less guilty that obliges him to steal.

Certain women are, it seems, being deceived by the pretence that laws are to be passed which will compel men to attend the periodical examination. What is the use of women clamouring for such a law as long as *men enact and enforce all our laws*? Men will never legislate themselves into the degradations and inconveniences of the compulsory periodical examination, and go to reside in hospitals as long as they are afflicted with disease. Will the Cantonment magistrate leave his judicial bench to go and sit in the Lock Hospital idly until he is no longer a source of danger to the community? Will the colonel of a regiment leave his soldiers to mutiny while he goes to reside in a Lock Hospital for a term of weeks? Such talk is the merest nonsense until only men of good morals control military affairs, and if they did there would be small demand for Lock Hospitals in India. The young soldiers could be readily trained to decency were it not for the utterly dishonouring views of life held by most of the high-titled officials over them. On this very proposal to examine men, the Secretary for War, Lord Lansdowne, said in the House of Lords, in the debate that took place May 17, 1897: "I have discussed that proposal with many high authorities, and I am bound to tell your lordships that the conclusion to which I am disposed to arrive is that this practice of regular inspection did not produce the desired effect; and that it was, on the contrary, regarded, and rightly regarded, by the men as a brutalizing and degrading practice." It has therefore been boldly determined and declared that men shall not be subjected to periodical examination (although there is not the faintest possibility of their ever being subjected to this humiliation by physicians of the opposite sex), for it is "brutalizing and degrading."[7] Yet it is these very men who are *directly* responsible for bringing disease back to England; for the native women do not go to England. The argument is, that since it brutalizes and degrades men to cause them to be examined, that they may not propagate disease in England, therefore the native women of India must be brutalized and degraded. It is useless to assert that the practice will not degrade women; we know that the moral nature of a woman is at least as susceptible of being injured by enforced immodesty as that of a man; in fact, as soon as it would serve any purpose in making a point in the interest of self, these very men would boldly proclaim, probably, the greater moral susceptibility of woman. It seems the extreme of servility for women to come to the front at this time, and in the face of the utter repudiation of all intention of examining men, declare for the examination of women. When men will not yield their dignity one jot, even for the sake of preserving the health of those women of England who are to become their future wives, what insolent hypocrisy for them to persuade deluded women to help them to bring women under practices so "degrading and brutalizing!" What infinite capacity of servility in the nature of women who will advocate such degrading, brutalizing treatment of women!

[7] When Lieut-General Lord Sandhurst was questioned before the Royal Commission of 1871 as to the advisability of soldiers being periodically examined by male physicians, he replied that he preferred to treat his soldiers "as reasonable men, not as brutes." Let women show at least equal consideration for women.

But, we may be asked, Shall women show no concern for the "innocent wives and children" of diseased men? Again we ask, Which wives and which children—the British or the Indian? There are hundreds of such wives and children who have been forsaken by husbands and fathers. There is almost a nation of Eurasians who curse the day they were given an unwelcome existence. And their mothers, in large numbers, were honestly married, to their best belief and intention. Here are the *real* wives and the *real* children in the sight of a just God, and to them should England's attention be first turned. The chaklas hold many such unwilling prisoners, left there by treacherous husbands and fathers. Some day this wife of the officer or soldier will be turned out to perish of the disease her system could no longer throw off, and the children will either be retained as soldiers' prostitutes or sent out to share the fate of the diseased mother. The women of England are being besought to turn their eyes on the future wives of British officers and soldiers; it would be for England's lasting good would they but persistently keep their eyes on the British officers' and soldiers' *present* wives and children in the far-off East. Were attention more persistently called to the Indian wife of the British soldier, there would be much less likelihood of his finding opportunity to entrap an innocent wife in the home-land.

It was suggested, in the first instance, by Sir George White, successor to Lord Roberts as Commander-in-Chief of the forces in India, and re-incorporated in the despatch of the Secretary of State as to immediate steps to be taken to check venereal disease, that female medical assistants be employed to conduct the examinations. It is our belief that respectable women-physicians wish to treat disease—not prostitution. Even if such were given the full control of Lock Hospitals, which is not likely, we wonder how many would like to return to their own country bearing certificates for faithful service, such as Mahaldarni Ezergee of the Cantonment of Rawal Pindi displayed to us with such evident pride, that she had been trained in other besides the ordinary duties of a mahaldarni: "The soldiers were remarkably healthy while the prostitutes were under her charge." Again, another officer had testified: "Few soldiers were in the hospital while the women were under her care." The surgeon of the regiment had testified: "Disease has been reduced to a minimum among the soldiers," while the women were under Ezergee, "superintendent of the prostitutes." This is what Lady Cook describes in a recent American periodical as "ministrations to women," while the certificates show that everything that was done was valued only as it protected the soldiers in vice; the indications as to the health of the women are never once even commented upon—all the work for women was done *with reference to men*. This being the fact, it is no wonder that in the official reply from India, dated May 18, 1897, and signed by the Viceroy, Sir George White, and others, it is declared that "It is doubtful whether the women possessing the necessary medical qualifications, and of a status sufficiently good to preclude the possibility of their receiving bribes from the women they have to examine, would be willing to undertake the work."[8]

[8] Perhaps they had in mind such a case as the woman we interviewed at Cantonment Bareilly. Her father was Scotch, she said—her mother, Portuguese; she had been trained by Dr. C——. She went every day to the brothels and examined the women. *She owned the brothels,* and resided with an official to whom she was not married. (See page 133, Departmental

As regards the examination of the women, we take a chapter out of the history of our India work, in illustration, as recorded in our Journal:

> MEERUT, India, February 8, 1892.
>
> At half-past seven this morning we went down the Sudder Bazaar to the neighbourhood of the Lock Hospital, it being examination day. The building is well placed for observation, being at a point where five streets meet, and several other streets run close by. The hospital is a foreign bungalow with a verandah in front, inclosed in a high brick wall. Already the girls, in gaudy apparel and flashy jewelry, were assembling, and in a few moments we counted thirty girls standing or sitting around, outside the building and outside the gate in the street. They came walking and riding in *ekkas* (native carts), and two loads came in cabs. Some of them had several miles to come from the Rest Camp. The vehicles waited for them across the street, under the shade trees. The girls went in by twos or threes, as summoned. A tall native policeman stood about, apparently to keep order. The street was one of Meerut's busiest thoroughfares. Men and boys lounged here and there, and even tiny children looked on with interest and curiosity. At one time we noticed not less than twenty-five men and boys gathered about and discussing the scene. A police station was close by, and an unusual number of men lingered in front of it, discussing the women, as their glances and manners indicated. One Eurasian woman brought a girl, evidently held as a slave to make money for her; she seemed reluctant to even trust her girl to go alone into the hospital, when her turn came; and as soon as she emerged again, seized her and led her away, the policemen shouting after her in derision, "Mem Sahib! Mem Sahib!" (the name for "lady," applied, as a rule, to white women), to which the Eurasian gave no response.

About a hundred women were examined that morning, waiting their turn on the public street, while the crowd gathered round to discuss the women kept by the Government for British soldiers. No wonder the Commander-in-Chief has decided that the female medical assistants who could be induced to manage such an affair would hardly be "sufficiently good to preclude the possibility of their receiving bribes." The Lock Hospitals of the Orient, as we studied them in many Cantonments of India, and also in Singapore and Hong Kong, are for the treatment of prostitution rather than for the treatment of disease, for the reason that only those who could be quickly restored to health to go on in their occupation are likely to be retained any length of time for treatment. We have already referred to the practice of turning cases of secondary, or advanced, disease out of the Cantonment. The position at the head of one of these hospitals is not likely to tax one's scientific resources much beyond instructing the native women how to perform ablutions, so strongly urged by Lord Roberts in his Circular Memorandum, in administering

---

Committee Report, 1893.)

douches, and in diagnosticating and keeping in hospital all cases of catamenia. We do not marvel if male surgeons have grown tired of the monotonous round, and with a seeming burst of generosity propose to give the position to medical women; particularly, if by such "generous" expressions of appreciation for the usefulness of women, they can lead over-credulous fine ladies into the conclusion that at last all the objections to the C. D. Acts have been met.

In spite of holding a degrading position the verdict of the world is "A man's a man for a' that"; but not so the woman who connects herself with an Eastern Lock Hospital—her dignity would never sustain the shock. Already the official conclusion is that no woman of intelligence or honesty would accept such a position. Women cannot afford to become the scavengers of the profession. We remember interviewing an Englishwoman in charge of a very large Lock Hospital in an Eastern city; and after this we went directly to the adjoining general hospital. We were welcomed by the nurses and treated most cordially until we mentioned, with design, the Englishwoman at the neighbouring hospital, and that we had been talking with her. A frozen response abruptly ended further sociability, and we learned thus that even underling nurses of other hospitals held themselves as in a position to snub the chief superintendent of a Lock Hospital in the East.

From the time that the abominable nature of the Contagious Diseases Acts of England and India were made known, and the Acts held up to public execration and outlawed, like a condemned criminal, this System has gone seeking a new *alias* that its identity might be hidden from the inconvenience of exposure. Many times these laws have been unmasked, and they have never been able to survive the exposure of their real name, which was at the first, "Contagious Diseases Acts."

Over and over again has this criminal Law, when caught sneaking about, denied his real name. Like a fatal birthmark, which no power can eradicate, so this abomination has its birthmark, which, when seen, fixes the identity beyond all question. That birthmark is *the compulsory examination of women*. This cannot be made to serve the desired purpose without all the essential features of the C. D. Acts. It makes not the slightest difference whether the law is called the Health Act, as in Australia, Getz's *Projet de Loi*, as in Norway, the Women's and Girls' Protection Ordinance, as at Singapore, the Cantonment Acts or the Cantonments Act, or what not—the test of the law, as to its identity with the old infamous C. D. Acts, is, whether women are obliged to submit to compulsory examination. "In fact, the compulsory examination of women *is* the C. D. Acts." Let this one point be put into law, and all the rest goes without saying. The battle has always raged around this one central point.

To prove that the compulsory examination of women necessitates the regulations that always attend it, let us suppose that in a community this one point is provided for by law, and that the officers of the law are left to enforce the measure, by whatever regulations are necessary:—

> The law demands merely that impure women must be examined regularly for the protection of the public health.
>
> But the police officer sees at once that to secure this point a

list must be kept of the women, when examined, that notice of requirement can be sent to those not coming voluntarily. Thus *registration* of prostitutes comes to pass.

But after examination, those found diseased must be placed by themselves for treatment. Thus a hospital for prostitutes is established.

Then provision must be made to compel those who are unwilling to attend the examinations to do so, for it has been the invariable experience that few women will go regularly for examination unless compelled to do so, and also there must be means of enforcing them to remain in hospital. Thus the hospital becomes a *Lock Hospital,* and *fines and imprisonments* are imposed on delinquents.

But compulsion cannot be secured without the aid of the police and the magistrate, and it is most difficult to follow up women, prove their identity, hale them to examination and to Lock Hospital without being able to keep them located in one tolerated quarter or house where they may be found—hence *segregation* is introduced; and this is also done to keep women with whom association is supposed to be safe—because under constant medical and police surveillance—separate from those with whom it is supposed to be a risk to associate.

Now we discover that the compulsory periodical examination of women of impure life, when carried out in actual operation, creates a necessity for all the essential features of every C. D. Act that has ever been known, namely: *Compulsory examination; Registration; Lock Hospitals; Fines and Imprisonments; Police Surveillance; Segregation.*

Yet another thing is needful for the operation of this law requiring compulsory periodical examination, namely, measures for extending the operation of the law, so that, as new women are likely to become a source of contamination, they also may be brought under its operation, and for the practical and easy operation of the measure, compelled to take up their residence in segregated quarters. *This is the special field of activity in the operation of the law,* and is a deadly menace to the most ordinary liberties of women. People will loudly advocate that "something must be done" to confine the houses of ill-fame to certain quarters of a city, without the slightest care as to how it is done, so long as they need not become intimately acquainted with a disagreeable subject; they will advocate measures of the most deadly consequences to others more defenceless than themselves, and to the ultimate moral tone of the very society in which they move, and yet heartlessly refuse to consider the responsibility that rests upon them for their conduct. "Something must be done," they say, and the police force must attend to the details; they are too loathsome even to be considered, yet they refuse to understand that these very loathsome details which they require the police to work out *must utterly ruin the character of the police* into whose hands they have betrayed all the decent rights of womanhood.

What does it mean to women for men to assume the right to arrest all suspicious characters and oblige them to live in a certain house or street, and to appear at the examinations at the Lock Hospitals? Let the banker sitting in his bank, or the merchant in his shop, consider what it would mean for him to be accosted in his own place of business, taken off immediately to the Lock Hospital, examined, and if the doctor so ordered, sent immediately into exile in a hospital for libertines, with no chance to set his house in order or to defend his character from the charge of being a libertine! And even if the charge were true would he not think the punishment too severe? And then, suppose it were the case that, at the end of the imprisonment in the hospital, he were required to reside for the rest of his days in a certain street? This is *exactly* what is done with women when once the principle is set up that compulsory periodical examinations must take place. But the reply is, No women of property or consequence would ever be so treated. Very true; yet are not these often utterly profligate? Certainly. So this is a law which will be operated only in the case of the lowly. Yes, it is a piece of legislation on the part of the mighty to degrade and rob the daughters of the poor of their most ordinary rights, and it deserves the *most extreme execration* that human language is capable of, on that very account. The day has passed by when it is safe to try to enunciate such sentiments among a free people. "What are the women making all this row about?" said one of the daily journals of London, during our India work; "no *high-born* ladies will ever be put to inconvenience by such a law." Ah! that was one of the principal reasons why such a row was made.

What does it mean to arrest a suspected case and send her to the segregated quarter for residence, where any man can assume the right to insult her and demand entrance at her door at any hour? It means that the law takes hold of a woman who may have occasionally done wrong and forces her to do wrong habitually; for after segregation no one will give her honest work. That law is radically wicked which confirms a human being into a habitual breaker of one of God's ten commandments.

And supposing the girl has not actually done wrong, but has conducted herself imprudently, and brought just suspicion on herself? To put her under the ban of such a law means to create a prostitute by law. That law is radically wrong which can be operated with such deadly effect on society as to actually create evil. Yet everywhere that the C. D. Acts have been operated such cases have occurred. The mayor of a city in South Africa told us that when a proposition for the introduction of these regulations was being entertained by the City Council of that place, and every effort was made to secure his approval, he was one day accosted by an alderman on the street, who plucked him by the sleeve, and pointing out a perfectly respectable-looking woman who was passing by, said, "Now, if we could get our law we could get that woman." He started back in horror, thinking to himself, "And if he could get his clutches on that woman by such a law, why not on any woman?"

Policemen are not supposed to be infallibly virtuous; and supposing they could be bribed or blackmailed? A policeman in Queensland confessed that he had taken a bribe to deliver a pretty girl over to the power of a libertine by having her registered as a common prostitute, and that he carried out the dastardly crime. A Christian woman in Cape Colony heard of the arrest as a common prostitute of a virtuous girl of her acquaintance, and went to the court to secure her release. There was a keeper of a house of ill-fame whom she recognised, who came to make accusation against the girl. The Christian worker appealed to a policeman, whom she knew as a church-member and a man of good repute, to stand with her for the girl's defence; but the evil woman took him to one side and she distinctly overheard her threaten to blast his reputation if he interfered. The magistrate took the word of this evil woman, which was corroborated by the falsehoods of the policeman, and in spite of her protestations, the girl was registered.

Another case was told us by a Wesleyan minister's wife; it occurred in England, before the repeal of the Acts. Her most intimate early friend, a lovely young Christian girl, had a brother who quarrelled with a policeman who threatened revenge. He watched his opportunity, arrested the sister, and gave his oath that she was a common prostitute; she was forced through the examination and registered, and when at last found by her brother, was a raving maniac as a result of the day's awful experience, and died shortly afterward in a madhouse. We might multiply the instances we have ourselves personally heard on good authority, and relate some of the many cases known to the history of the movement for repeal, but there is no space for further enlargement.

Again we say there is something radically wrong with this law, when women can be so fearfully wronged in its operation, should the police officers and magistrates be either wicked or weak. Practically such a law delivers the reputation of women wholly over to the power of the police. But, some one says, let no case be settled on suspicion; let proof be brought. The question arises, How secure the proof? In India it was considered sufficient by Lord Roberts to teach the soldiers that it was "a point of honour" to save other soldiers from disease by informing against women; but it has frequently been observed that the soldier will usually point out another woman rather than the one he has actually associated with, and women are haled to the examinations who may never have seen the informant before. It detracts nothing from the peril of girls and women when the uncorroborated testimony of a self-confessed libertine can be used against them, and the frequency with which evil men will combine to utterly break down the testimony of a young woman in case of seduction, and the unblushing testimony of these men to their own shameful conduct, which is often treated as a joke by the magistrate, shows that the reputation of a woman is no safer in the hands of a combination of libertines. Nothing is much more difficult than to actually *prove* a woman a prostitute, and short of absolute proof, the thought of registration, segregation, imprisonment in a Lock Hospital, etc., is intolerable.

Again, a single act of fornication does not prove prostitution, and how many acts shall constitute proof? Practically, these are things that the law never has considered at all; but wherever the compulsory examination has been established, secret information from libertines is received and acted upon with little question as to its veracity, and the whole system has immediately degenerated into a costly effort on the part of the State, paid for by the taxes of respectable people, to pander to the wishes of libertines, and keep the houses of ill-fame filled with attractive and healthy inmates, and thus the State becomes itself the great purveyor of vice. We have said before repeatedly, and say again, that there is no real evidence that prostitution has been made safer by the periodical examination of women, because the false security in vice greatly increases the amount of vice, which is itself the cause of the diseases in question. Not only does correct reason testify to this, but also statistics uphold this statement.

We have now shown that the compulsory examination of women brings into existence, of necessity, every feature of what is commonly called the C. D. Acts; and that, as that compulsory examination is of itself a sin, so every feature of the enactments necessary to carry out that law is at each step liable to fearful abuse, and the system as a whole is ruinous to the morals of any community.

V.

PLEADING FOR THE OPPRESSED.

MANY times in the course of our conversations with the little women of India we had promised before leaving them to do what we could to secure relief and help for them. In the simplicity of their faith and lack of practical knowledge, several of them had ventured to intimate that we might go to England and see the Queen, and tell her their troubles. "For," they said, "the Queen does not countenance it; for she has daughters of her own, and she cares for her daughters in India." "The Queen is a woman, and we also are women, and our shame is the Queen's shame; and for us to be exposed is as though the Queen were exposed; it is a shame for women to be so treated when a woman is Queen."

At Peshawar, at Lucknow, and at Meerut, the girls had held us at parting until they had solemnly lifted their eyes to heaven and asked God's blessing on us, and asked Him to help us to help them to get deliverance from their oppression. God heard the prayer, although their knowledge of Him was probably very obscure. The sacred promises we gave them and gave Him to help them, can never be set aside without bringing guilt on our own souls. They depend upon us to voice their sorrows and plead their cause, by solemn compact with them and God. May He keep us faithful to the trust!

We carefully prepared the report of our investigations and forwarded this to Miss Forsaith, of London, Secretary of the British Committee of the Federation for the Abolition of State Regulation of Vice. Then as the summer was too far advanced to hold any meetings in India, we proceeded to Australia, New Zealand, and Tasmania, in the interests of our regular work. But in the early part of the year 1893 we were summoned to England to give evidence in person concerning the condition of things in the Cantonments of India, which went to prove that, although the C. D. Acts had been ordered to be repealed, the same state of things was being maintained, under the Cantonments Act of 1889, and that the resolution of the House of Commons of 1888 had been disregarded.

A Departmental Committee was appointed by the Government to receive our evidence. This Committee was composed of Mr. George W. E. Russell, M.P., Under-Secretary of State for India (Chairman); The late Right Hon. Sir James Stansfeld, M.P.; General Sir Donald M. Stewart, Bart., G.C.B., Commander of the Forces in India, before Lord Roberts; Sir James Peile, K.C.S.I.; Mr. H. J. Wilson, M.P., with Major-General O. R. Newmarch, C.S.I., as Secretary. The first sitting of the Committee, at the India Office, London, was April 11, 1893. Before this Departmental

Committee we appeared day after day until the full report of our statements had been made. In the course of the giving of this evidence, we described with accuracy the records which we had seen in the various Lock Hospitals of the ten Cantonments visited when in India, and a telegram was sent by the chairman of the Committee, Mr. George Russell, giving our description and requesting that these records be impounded by the India Government and forwarded to London for reference. Then our full statement was despatched to India for reply.

Meanwhile, Lord Roberts, who had returned to England, had been interviewed by a reporter of *The Christian Commonwealth*, who placed before him some of our statements regarding the Cantonments of India. Lord Roberts pronounced them "simply untrue," and declared that he had recently made a tour of investigation through the Cantonments, and knew that our statements were false. His open charges of falsehood against us were heralded throughout the Empire, and freely discussed by the Press from the time they were made in April to the time of our second appearance before the Committee in August.

Upon the receipt of our evidence in India there was a Special Commission appointed by the Indian Government, to collect evidence in refutation of our charges, two members of it being instructed to proceed to England therewith, and to give personal testimony in behalf of the Indian Government.

The Special Commission did not come before the Committee until August, and we spent much of the interim in addressing public meetings throughout Great Britain, and arousing interest in the subject. Many large and important meetings were also addressed by such well-known leaders as Mrs. Josephine Butler, the late Sir James Stansfeld, M.P., Mr. Henry J. Wilson, M.P., and Mrs. H. J. Wilson, Mr. James Stuart, M.P., and many other Members of Parliament. At the annual conferences and assemblies of the various denominations, the subject was taken up; many ladies of the Women's Liberal Federation and of the British Women's Temperance Association, and of other bodies, presented the matter in their meetings, and ministers of all denominations lent their help. At all these meetings resolutions were passed condemning legalized vice, and from all of them memorials were sent to the Government, protesting against the condition of things prevalent in the Cantonments of India. It was truly touching to witness the intense interest manifested in the subject by the common people, the class from whom the soldiers are so largely drawn, and for whose sake military officials claimed that it was necessary to establish the chakla system. The mothers and fathers of British lads had their own opinion as to what was necessary for their boys.

"I'll buy him off! I'll buy him off!" exclaimed one woman to us, with streaming eyes, at the close of one of our meetings. "My boy enlisted to go to India without my consent and then repented, and I thought it would teach him a lesson to compel him to abide by his word. He has already got as far as Gibraltar, I think; but I'll send the money and buy him off. I cannot consent to let him go out under officers who will teach him that vice is necessary." Another mother expressed great indignation at our statements regarding the temptations put in the way of young soldiers by their superiors, and declared she would write to her boy and obtain his contradiction of them. The reply came back, and the almost broken-hearted mother caused it to be conveyed to us, together with an exhortation that we should "cry aloud and spare not." It was to the following effect:

"Yes, mother, all those ladies say is true, and much more that they do not know, and you would hardly believe. I have been so harassed and persecuted that sometimes I have gone to the chakla, pretending to sin, but God knows I have not; it was the only way to escape their merciless persecution."

We have been informed many times that there were military officers who sneered at virtuous soldiers as lacking proper fighting qualities, and who deliberately fostered in their soldiers animal propensities, for the sake of the ferocity of disposition that attends licentiousness.

The names of the special Commissioners were: Mr. Denzil Ibbetson and Surgeon-Colonel J. Cleghorn, M.D., Inspector-General of Civil Hospitals throughout the Punjab. In addition to these witnesses from India and ourselves, Lord Roberts, Quartermaster-General Chapman, and Mr. Hyslop Bell, of Darlington, were called before the Departmental Committee to give evidence.

The statements of Lord Roberts and of General Chapman, who were called before the Departmental Committee in August, proved to be matters of intense interest, especially as regarded their disagreement as to Lord Roberts' knowledge of the Infamous Memorandum. Lord Roberts testified that, when the Resolution of 1888 was carried in the House of Commons not permitting the compulsory examination of women or the licensing of prostitution, he understood those measures to mean *abolition*, not modification, of measures for the regulation of prostitution, and proceeded accordingly. The Resolution meant the abolishing of the periodical examination, of licensing, of compulsion, of regulation, etc. He declared that he knew nothing of the Infamous Memorandum which had been issued in his name, and that he "entirely disapproved" of some of the contents of that circular, saying, "I certainly would not have approved of that part of the Circular which referred to providing them with pretty young women." Lord Roberts was confronted with a mass of evidence which he little expected. After his own sweeping contradictions of our statements, he was shown the report from the Cantonment of Meean Meer which the Special Commission had brought from India, and in which nearly every statement we had made was "admitted." Other *prima facie* evidence of the truth of our statements convinced him that our testimony was not to be broken down. As he left the Committee it was with the conviction that General Chapman was next to be called, and would give most disagreeable evidence against him as regarded the Infamous Memorandum and its authorship. Lord Roberts proceeded immediately to Scotland, and from thence wrote the following letter of apology:—

DUNBAR, Scotland, 11 August, 1893.

> Having read the reports of Mr. Ibbetson's Committee, in regard to the working of the Rules dealing with the abolition of Lock Hospitals, etc., in Cantonments in India, and also the reports of the officers commanding the seven stations which the Committee did not visit, I frankly admit that the statements of the two American missionary ladies, who made a tour through Upper In-

dia in the cold weather of 1891–92, for the purpose of inquiring into the matter, are in the main correct.

I hoped and believed that the orders issued to give effect to the Resolution of the House of Commons had been everywhere obeyed. In some stations the Rules have been strictly enforced, but in others it now turns out this has not been completely the case.

I deeply regret this, and I feel that an apology is due from me to the ladies concerned. This apology I offer unreservedly.

In doing so, I would remark that I think it would have been better if the missionary ladies had been commended to the care of the authorities in India. We could have assisted them to carry out the work on which they were engaged; omissions and shortcomings would have been remedied at the time; a great deal of unpleasantness would have been avoided; the ladies themselves would have found their task considerably lightened; and there would have been less chance of their drawing wrong deductions from some of the circumstances which came under their notice, as in sundry instances they would seem from Mr. Ibbetson's Committee Report to have done. This was owing, no doubt, to a want of knowledge of the language, and of the habits and customs of the people of India. ROBERTS.

This letter was accompanied by a short note to the Chairman requesting him to annex the letter of apology to the official report of the proceedings of the Committee.

A few days later General Chapman came before the Committee and testified with regard to the Circular Memorandum: "It was prepared at Simla, after the Commander-in-Chief [Lord Roberts] had completed his annual inspection, and had freely discussed with the officers in command the various measures which it was proposed to adopt." General Chapman described the manner in which it was done as follows: The Commander-in-Chief gave the instruction that the Circular be prepared; then it was drawn up by officials in the General's office under his supervision. The Surgeon-General was consulted; then the Circular was issued under the authority of the Commander-in-Chief. It was sent first to the Military Department of the Government of India, and then sent in every direction to all the authorities in India. He said he "could not have issued" the Circular "unless Lord Roberts had seen it; that would have been perfectly impossible." When questioned particularly as to Lord Roberts' knowledge of that part of the document which, as Lord Roberts expressed it, called for "pretty young women" to be provided for the soldiers, General Chapman said of these sentences: "He certainly did approve of them." When asked how it was that the Secretary of State laid the blame on him (General Chapman), in the House of Commons, he replied: "Sir John Gorst said it was necessary to put the blame on somebody, therefore he put it on me."

In the meantime a box had arrived from India containing the hospital records, which had been impounded by the Indian Government, on the request of the Chairman of the Committee, and they furnished a large quantity of *prima facie* evidence, in the very handwriting of the British officials. These books being placed in our hands, we were able to verify the statements we had given in evidence concerning these records, and were also able to place official documents before the Committee which disproved some of the statements which had been conveyed to England from India by the hand of the two Special Commissioners. As this well illustrates the utter unreliability of many Anglo-Indian official assertions, we will copy a condensed and simplified extract from the proceedings of that session of the Committee at which we placed official document against official document, and pointed out irreconcilable differences.

The reader must try to imagine us sitting in one of the spacious rooms of the India Office. At the head of an oval polished table sat Mr. Russell, the chairman; to his left sat General Newmarch, Sir Donald Stewart, and Sir James Peile. To the chairman's right sat the late Sir James Stansfeld, whose prerogative it was to conduct the examination; next to him were Mr. Casserley, Q.C., counsel for our side, and Henry J. Wilson, M.P. At the opposite end of the table from the chairman sat the stenographer and ourselves. It is to be understood that Mr. Stansfeld asks the questions and we answer:

> *Question*—We will pass to the book of requisition for tickets. [This was a book from which many leaves were torn, leaving counterfoils on which were memoranda signifying that the extracted leaves were given to the Cantonment Magistrate, calling for tickets for women, who were thereby certified as under the charge of the physician, and licensed to practise prostitution.]
>
> *Answer*—I have it.
>
> *Q.*—And you can number the counterfoils; how many requisitions to the Cantonment Magistrate for licensed tickets does it say on the 1st of May, 1892?
>
> *A.*—Twenty-one.
>
> *Q.*—Does it say on counterfoils of tickets in respect of the nineteen new requisitions on 15th June, 1892?
>
> *A.*—It does.
>
> *Q.*—Therefore that is evidence that the issue of tickets at any rate endured longer than May?
>
> *A.*—Yes, longer than the 1st of May; it shows that it continued until the 15th of June, 1892.
>
> *Q.*—At any rate, on the 15th of June a requisition was made for nineteen tickets?
>
> *A.*—Nineteen tickets.
>
> *Q.*—According to the Military Reports before us, page 18, on line 940: "Women were registered, tickets issued, and bi-month-

ly inspections made between March, 1890, and May, 1892; it was brought to my notice in May, 1892 that tickets were being issued to prostitutes in Meean Meer; I ordered the discontinuance of the practice at once, and it was reported to me on the 17th of May, 1892, that no registration of prostitutes in any form whatever then continued;" and it appears from what you have now produced, that at any rate requisitions were made as late as the 15th of June; that is so, is it not?

A.—Yes.

Q.—Of those requisitions on that date, the 15th of June, as well as on several other dates, do you find some, and how many, issued for the Royal Artillery Bazaar?

A.—I counted twenty that were for the Royal Artillery Bazaar women.

Q.—Have you seen the Report of the Commanding Officer for the regiment dated 19th June, 1893, and does it state that no tickets had been issued for the regiment since February, 1891?

A.—Yes, I saw that statement; it is page 2 of the supplementary sheet, line 95, under Meean Meer. The statement of Captain Goff, commanding the Royal Artillery. That note says, "No registration of prostitutes or issue of tickets in any form whatever has ever been carried out by the Royal Artillery since the present battery came to the station, February, 1891."

Q.—What you find is that twenty tickets were issued?

A.—It is since February, 1891, according to this book some twenty tickets have been issued for the Royal Artillery.

Q.—Up to what date?

A.—Up to June 15th, 1892.

Q.—You produce a ticket here which you obtained from one of the women; what was the date of that ticket; was not the date of the year 1892?

A.—It was dated 1892; that we procured at the Artillery Bazaar.

Q.—Did I understand you to say that you found twenty tickets were issued to the women of the Artillery?

A.—Yes, twenty counterfoils left are of the Royal Artillery.

Mr. Stansfeld to the Committee—That fact, which is testified to by the counterfoils of this book, is inconsistent with the statement of the Commanding Officer in his Report.

These are but a few of the many instances in which the official records sent to London for inspection, contradicted the testimony of military officers.

The first sitting of the Departmental Committee was April 11, its last sitting August 15, and its report was circulated in Parliament September 11, 1893.

With the acknowledgment from the Commander-in-Chief of the truth of our statements, a most sweeping victory had been gained for the cause; no under-official could very well dispute the word of the Commander-in-Chief of the army. Lord Roberts' remark that "the ladies themselves would have found their task considerably lightened" had they been "commended to the care of the authorities in India," was the source of a good deal of amusement on the part of our friends, and led to many a sarcastic comment on the part of the public press; some of which ran somewhat as follows: "As Lord Roberts freely admitted that he did not know these things, certainly had the ladies appealed to him they need not have come back so loaded with information; this would have greatly lightened their task." "As there was a regulation which allowed any suspicious characters to be expelled from the Cantonments without assigning a reason therefor, the application of this regulation would greatly have 'lightened their task,'" etc., etc.

What had been fully established by the evidence cannot be better expressed than in the recent utterance of the British Committee for the Abolition of State Regulation of Vice, *i.e.*:—

"The fact was fully established that the so-called voluntary system had been completely overridden by *extra-legal* practices, of which the provision placing, or interpreted to have placed, venereal diseases under the same rule as 'cholera, small-pox, diphtheria, or typhoid fever,' became the fulcrum or pivot." The thing which now remained to be done was to embody the Resolution of the House of Commons of 1888 in a law which must be passed by the Government of India, that could not be longer evaded or disobeyed. After much discussion and consideration, the Secretary of State for India directed that the Cantonment regulations which related to the removal to hospital of those persons suspected of contagious or infectious diseases, must be so altered as to admit of the treatment of contagious diseases due to vice in a manner that would not be liable to abuse of or injury to the reputation of women.

Accordingly the Cantonments Act of 1889 in so far as it provided for the compulsory examination of women suspected of contagious diseases due to vice, and their forcible detention in hospital under penalty of expulsion from the Cantonment, was altered to apply only to cholera, smallpox, diphtheria, or typhoid fever. This was done to protect the character and reputation of women, for it had been conceded on all sides that hitherto the only method practicable for getting hold of suspected women was on the information of male libertines, and that such persons when questioned as to the source of their contagion, generally sought to cover their own wrong-doing or protect their real partner in sin by accusing some other woman, often a perfectly innocent person.

This new Act, called the Cantonments Act Amendment Act, was passed on February 8, 1895. The point which was gained by the passage of this new Act was one of great importance, namely, that there were moral and social questions involved in the treatment of contagious diseases due to vice which could not be overlooked in the medical management of such disorders without serious consequences. It was, in the nature of the case, impossible to place these diseases on the same footing as other contagious disorders. The reasons for this position have been recently expressed very concisely and forcibly by the British Committee, in the following language:—

> "1. It casts no stigma on the name or character of a person to assert that he, or she, is affected with 'cholera, smallpox, diphtheria, or typhoid fever,' and it can be ascertained whether such statement be true without shock to the feelings of the most refined. The opposite is the case with venereal disease, in regard to which a mis-statement is a virtual libel, and a compulsory examination is an indecent outrage. 2. As regards the former classes of disease, no conceivable measures can have any moral bearing; whereas in the latter class compulsory (and in some of its relations, even voluntary) submission to examination or treatment has the gravest moral consequences both to the individual and to the community. 3. The procedure under the rules you propose is as follows: The medical officer is informed by a soldier that a certain woman is diseased. Believing that, he orders her for examination at the hospital. She may be perfectly honourable or perfectly healthy. In either case if she refuses to attend she is held to be diseased and is expelled from the Cantonment. We submit that the whole of this procedure, though it may be in words the same as in a case of cholera, is in fact utterly different in the means by which information is secured, in the nature of the evidence as to fact, and in the consequences to the woman who disputes the fact. The operation of the rules, so far as venereal disease is concerned, is not general.
>
> "In the Report of the Special Indian Commission appointed in 1893 by the Government of India to inquire into the working of the regulations, it is stated that so far as venereal disease is concerned the operation of the rules is 'practically confined by sheer force of circumstances to women.' . . . 'Even with regard to them information is difficult to obtain, for a man often does not know, and still oftener will not tell, which woman has diseased him.' . . . 'Except in the not infrequent cases where a woman herself applies for medical aid, this (*i.e.*, information necessary to proceed upon) can only be obtained from men who have been diseased by them.' It is clear, then, that a man, as the result of an admittedly immoral act, becomes an informer, and in many cases a false informer, upon whose testimony the State has to rely for submitting the woman to the most degrading process. We submit that there is no parallel between venereal disease and cholera, either in the procedure here indicated, or in the effect of that procedure on moral conduct, or in the position in which it places the State."

VI.

SOME ANGLO-INDIAN MORAL SENTIMENTS.

WE have referred to the discrepancies between the statements of Lord Roberts and of General Chapman; between Lord Roberts' first attempt to discredit our evidence and subsequent admission of its truth; between the records that had been kept at the Lock Hospitals which we visited in India and the statements sent home by the Special Commission. All these things must tend to weaken the faith of the public in Anglo-Indian representations. They all accord in spirit with the gross exaggerations which have been put forth, as though a veritable scourge of such diseases was at the door of England. As to the prevalence of disease, "Between fifty and sixty per cent. of our Indian army," is found to be, in actual fact, only *four and one-half per cent.* (see page 69), and "Thirteen per cent. annually invalided home hopelessly incurable," is found to be, in actual fact, only *one-ninth of one per cent.*

"Our power is being sapped—our race defiled—and we are forced to ask ourselves if no means can be devised of stopping so gigantic an infliction." What does this mean in exact figures? How "gigantic" in reality is this infliction? The official figures of the very document which was meant to originate the alarm, the Report of the Departmental Committee of 1897 shall testify. The latest year reported in this document is 1895, and as the law which effectually forbade the compulsory examination of women was passed on February 8, 1895, the figures show the result only of *less than eleven months* covering the existence of that law. Out of a force of 71,031 soldiers in India nineteen more men were sent home to England, "hopelessly incurable" from vice, in 1895 than in the year 1894. *Nineteen cases* represent the size of this "gigantic infliction" which has been made the occasion of raising such a cry of alarm, and a demand for the return to licensed prostitution and the re-enslavement of thousands of native women by compulsory examination measures.

In the year 1894, 111 men were sent home invalided from this cause, and in 1895, 130 men were sent home—an increase of nineteen cases. We do not wish to minimize the evil of even these few cases; but is a decent nation prepared to hazard an attempt to purchase immunity from disease by plunging into brazen defiance of God's seventh commandment? What about the "gigantic [immoral] infliction" of the atheistic assumption that chastity is a sanitary failure, and fornication a necessity? There is no comparison between the "gigantic infliction" upon England of a teaching to defy God's commandments in the fancied interests of physical health, and the presence of nineteen additional diseased soldiers in a population of thirty-five millions.

But if we continue the study of the table of statistics found on page 9 of the Report referred to, we find that eighty-four more men were sent home to England in 1894 for diseases due to vice, than during the previous year, 1893. If the increase of disease in 1895 over 1894 is to be attributed to the Amendment Act of 1895, to what shall we attribute the much more pronounced increase of 1894 over 1893? Again, there were forty more men sent home invalided in 1891 than in 1890; and forty-three more sent home in 1888 than in 1887, and none of these years were under the Amendment Act of 1895. Therefore it is proved that variations and increases have taken place that have had nothing to do with the Amendment Act of 1895, which, when it serves the object of advocates of licensed vice, is held wholly responsible for the insignificant variation of an increase of nineteen cases. In view of these facts, we must declare our solemn conviction that the agitation for a return to legalized prostitution in India is not due to any feeling of alarm on account of the spread of contagion in the case of the *originators* of the agitation, but that an attempt is being made to frighten an unwilling Christian public into a reluctant consent to return to a system which regards the whoremonger as a necessity, the commandments of God a farce, and the slave trade in women an important part of the business of the State.

Life in India does not tend to the elevation of British morals, and this not because of the climate, as some contend. The industrial conditions are all against good morals, and are closely analogous to the conditions that prevailed in the Southern States of America before the Civil War. Wages are so low in India as to constitute the native the virtual slave of the Anglo-Saxon. By means of the pitiful wages paid for work, not one-half the comfort is provided by white masters to Indian servants that was secured to the black men in America, by the few of those owners of slaves who were really humane. The very fact that the slave was a rather scarce article and a good price paid for him in America, made it to the interest of his owner to look after his health and comfort to a certain extent. We are not defending slavery—it is an abomination in the sight of God, whether it exists under the disguise of abnormally low wages or shows itself openly; and slavery is always a greater moral curse to the master than to the oppressed. England virtually owns a whole nation of slaves in her control of India, and the effect of this fact upon the morals of that country will depend wholly upon whether she rules to redeem her subjects or to enrich herself. The worst feature of all in slavery is the appropriation of women by their masters. And this form of villainy is always excusing itself by slandering the oppressed women.

"This life is not *a life of shame* in the sense in which this is true in England. Most of these women are prostitutes by caste and *can feel no desire to give it up*," says the Report of the Special Commission of 1893. "They are accepted as safeguards to society, and are not themselves ashamed of their calling," says a high military officer. "They feel no shame about this; they are never recruited from seduced girls, as in England," says another of these high and mighty officers, who know so much better how these girls feel and what they desire than do the poor slaves themselves. To be sure, they sob and cry and petition for deliverance, and protest their outraged feelings against the examinations; but that merely proves what hypocrites they are, and how cleverly they can play a part. "They are as artful as a waggon-load of monkeys," said one Anglo-Indian to us; the "most vicious and degraded of the population," says another. And yet they are, many of them, the offspring of British men. One would imagine them gray-haired in the service of Satan, from these accounts, and yet General Viscount Frankfort states in the Report of the Special Commission of 1893: "It is roughly estimated that 50 per cent. [of the girls of the chakla] are of the age of fourteen to sixteen or so;" and in reply to our evidence as to some of the girls being as young as "from fifteen to sixteen years of age," Major General Sir W. Elles, K.C.B., replies, "The probability is that prostitution is practised at even younger ages than this." In reply to our further statement that many girls are kept at the point of starvation, are always in debt, and cannot escape on this account, even if otherwise the way might be open, Colonel T. G. Crawley, commanding Allahabad District, makes the following calculation (page 360, Departmental Committee Report of 1893):—

> "It stands to reason that the women could not be in debt, for if a woman only received six men daily for twenty-three days in a month, at the rate of only four annas [about fourpence] per visit, that would represent thirty-four rupees eight annas, and even allowing one-fourth of this to go to the mahaldarni, rent two rupees, and food at the rate of four annas daily for thirty days, a woman would have fully seventeen rupees [a little more than one pound] a month clear."

This for the health of British soldiers and their "future wives" and "unborn offspring" in England! and fifty per cent. of these victims from fourteen to sixteen years of age! And will women physicians be induced to attempt the task of keeping these mere children in health under such conditions?

Anglo-Indian sentiment would not long content itself with the loss of its highly prized C. D. Acts. The military officials had professed to abrogate them when they hid them away under the cloak of the Indian Cantonment Acts, and then again when they hid them under the cloak of the Cantonments Act of 1889; but they were at last fairly caught by the Cantonments Act Amendment Act of 1895, which tore away from them the pretence of "only treating this as any other contagious disease."

Regulation had been in operation in India, in one form or another, for the largest part of a century, and statistics show a steady increase of disease, with slight variations, during all that time. And the Army Sanitary Commission, the highest British medical authority, had in 1894 pronounced this prolonged experiment with licensed vice a failure, in the following unequivocal language:—

> "The facts, so far as we can ascertain them, lead us to the conclusion that a compulsory Lock Hospital system in India has proved a failure, and that its re-institution cannot consequently be advocated on sanitary grounds. In stating this conclusion, we may add that we are merely repeating the opinions which the Army Sanitary Commission have uniformly held, that venereal

> diseases in the army of India could not be repressed by such restrictive measures, and in support of this statement, we may refer to the Memoranda on the Indian Sanitary Reports which have issued from this office for many years."

Yet a Departmental Committee was secured in November, 1896, by Anglo-Indian influence brought to bear upon the Government, to examine into the matter and report on the prevalence of diseases due to vice; and it reported, as was expected, in favour of a return to the system of legalized vice. The Departmental Committee reported at the beginning of the year 1897, on statistics no later than the year 1895. Now the Cantonments Act Amendment Act became a law in India, February 8, 1895, and how much time elapsed before this Amendment Act came into *practical operation* remains yet to be shown; yet an attempt is made to show that incalculable mischief has been done during these eleven months of the actual existence of the law which abolished licensed prostitution. The official statistics of which they make use do not at all justify the calculations and conclusions they have drawn therefrom.

At about the time of the report of the Departmental Committee, there was formed in England an association with the object of securing the re-establishment of legalized vice in India. The names of high British military officials make up its membership list, in large part. The association printed a pamphlet, based upon the Departmental Committee's Report in favour of a return to the old conditions, a Report that was calculated to frighten the public, if possible, into acceding to their demands, on the supposition that a fearful scourge was upon them, and that no time was to be lost in getting it under check. Then Lord George Hamilton, on March 26, 1897, sent a dispatch to the Government of India, calling attention to the Report of the Departmental Committee, and ordering stricter measures for the suppression of diseases due to vice, but adding: "There must be no provision of women, . . . no registration, . . . no compulsory examination of women," etc., but urging that it was "imperatively necessary that this disease should not be exempted from the measures adopted to prevent the spread of other contagious diseases." "If there be any compulsion, it is precisely of the same kind as that which has been accepted as necessary and enforced without any objection in the case of diphtheria or typhoid fever."

Now the first quotation given effectually contradicts the second, at the point of the compulsory examination of women; and such instructions were, in fact, a virtual order to repeal the Amendment Act of 1895, very covertly expressed, and so it was recognised immediately by the British Committee for the Abolition of State Regulated Vice, which promptly issued a memorial on the subject addressed to Lord George Hamilton, Secretary of State for India.[9]

On April 21, 1897, there appeared in the London *Times* part of a letter from Lady Henry Somerset to Lord George Hamilton, in which she "expresses grati-

[9] "Lord George Hamilton himself instigated disregard of his own command by sanctioning the repeal of the law which had embodied it, upon a pretext so grotesquely irrelevant that an admission of its ingenuousness is tantamount to a charge of imbecility against the sanctioning Minister." —*The Shield*, November, 1897.

fication at finding incorporated in a document of such importance a statement of inspiring and controlling principles." She notes with satisfaction the "inclusion of this disease among other contagious diseases," as the "only rational and scientific principle on which its eradication can be attempted." "It is not however, proposed to carry out this principle to its full logical result; and herein lies the point on which she finds herself at issue with Lord George Hamilton." At the end of the letter is affixed the system of legislation best suited to the end, in the opinion of Lady Henry Somerset, and it will be seen at a glance that her propositions would indeed carry out the principle to its full, logical end. A special importance attaches itself to these propositions, because of the strategic position held by Lady Henry Somerset as president of the British Women's Temperance Association of England, and first vice-president of the World's W.C.T.U., and her action put her in absolute opposition to the purity department of both those societies.

The scheme proposed by Lady Henry Somerset is here given in her own words:

> "1. A quarter of each Cantonment should be reserved for such women as are permitted to remain in camp, and all such women should be compelled to remain in houses or rooms specifically reserved to each by a registered number. The admission of men to this quarter should be strictly supervised.
>
> "2. No woman should be allowed to remain in this quarter unless periodically examined by properly qualified women doctors.
>
> "3. No soldier should be allowed to enter this quarter without having undergone a like examination and having the same report.
>
> "4. A register should be kept recording the name of each soldier entering the quarter, the number of the house to which he goes, and the date of such entry.
>
> "5. On any woman being found to be diseased in this quarter, or on any soldier found to be suffering in like manner, all such persons that the registered visits show to have rendered themselves liable to contagion should be put in quarantine until such time as their immunity can be verified.
>
> "6. All consorting with women outside this quarter should render the offender liable to severe penalty."[10]

The *Shield*, official organ of the British Committee for the Abolition of State Regulated Vice, in its issue of May, 1897, comments as follows upon this scheme:

> "The suggestions above quoted embody the most complete State Regulation of prostitution which we have ever seen described, in its baldest and most absolute form, and imply the most

[10] Lady Henry Somerset addressed a letter to Lord George Hamilton, January 27th, 1898, withdrawing these propositions. But alas! such a tardy withdrawal cannot undo the mischief wrought to the native girls of India by the repeal of the Cantonment Acts Amendment Act of 1895 (see Appendix C).

> complete identification of the State with the purely animal side of the matter which has ever been proposed. They seem to emanate from a mind influenced for the time solely by the idea of equality between man and woman, to the exclusion of other considerations. Such proposals seem indeed to make the sexes equal, but it is an equality of unspeakable degradation for both."

On May 14 and 17 occurred a debate in the House of Lords on the question of a return to legalized prostitution in India, in which reference was made to Lady Henry Somerset's letter in *The Times*, and to another memorial which was shortly "to be made public," and which was signed by a very large number of ladies, as an indication that women were no longer, as formerly, opposed to the system of State Regulation of Vice.[11]

On May 25 *The Times* published the text of this Memorial, which is signed by ladies of the aristocracy, together with a few other prominent women, numbering in all one hundred and twenty-three.

The Government of India proceeded at once to repeal the Cantonments Act Amendment Act of 1895, in the Viceregal Council held at Simla July 8, which action had received the approval of Lord George Hamilton by telegram, July 6, 1897. Since that day, therefore, the military authorities have been set free to return to the establishment of brothel slavery, the registration and compulsory examination of women, the employment of procuresses, and all the infamies which we have described as existing when we visited India in 1892.

Meanwhile, the women of Great Britain have arisen in mighty protest, and a Memorial signed by 61,437 women of the United Kingdom, addressed to Lord George Hamilton, as representative of Her Majesty's Government, was presented at the India Office on Saturday, July 31, 1897, as follows:

> "It declares the unaltered and unalterable hostility of the signatories to every form of State Regulation of Immorality, whether embodied in the system which was known as the Contagious Diseases Acts or in any other form, including the slightly modified and more subtle garb of certain Indian Cantonment rules.
>
> "It objects to the principle of all such legislation, a principle based on the assumption of the necessity of vice. It opposes the system in all its forms, because it inevitably becomes, in regard to women, an engine of the most shameful oppression, removing the guarantees of personal liberty which the law has established, and putting their reputation, their freedom, and their persons absolutely in the power of the police; while in respect to those women who come immediately under its action, it cruelly violates the feelings of those whose sense of shame is not wholly lost, and

[11] Additional colour was given to this, later, by Lady Henry Somerset placing the name of Lord Roberts (author of the "Infamous Circular Memorandum," the history of which we have given in chapters 1 and 5) on the Advisory Board of the Duxhurst Inebriate Home of the B.W.T.A., at the Annual Conference of the Association in June, 1897.

further brutalizes even the most abandoned.

"The Memorialists, while deploring the existence of disease and favourable to moral methods of diminishing it, urge that no permanent diminution of disease will ever be attained by measures which do not strike primarily at the vice itself, and express the hope that the Government of our country will be withheld from the crime of ever again entering into any compact with evil by its attempted regulation."

We have been deeply impressed with the thought that, in our search for the cause of the present moral confusion, we need to go further back than the influence of high-placed military officers and ladies of the aristocracy. There have arisen occasions in the past when the Christian public have been able to successfully resist the invasions of materialistic and immoral counsels, although they were advocated by the rich and mighty. Only the blind can be led by the blind: those who have clear vision will not follow such leadership. Whence this far-reaching influence, then, which has blinded the eyes of so many? Alas! these are the days of a paralysed faith, and faith is as indispensable a faculty of the human mind as is reason.

The re-enthronement of faith is the need of the hour. Science we have, and scholarship: but hesitancy and doubt rule the scientific spirit, and timidity is the vice of the scholar. The soldier who hesitates and doubts and grows timid will not win a single battle. His must be the prophetic spirit of faith which "laughs at impossibilities, and cries, It shall be done." But the Church militant has been ridiculed out of the warrior spirit, and has laid aside its mightiest weapon, faith; and as to leadership, many are pointing to science and scholarship and crying, "These be thy gods, O Israel!" Science and scholarship have their place and their power, but they are not the Christian's mightiest weapons. Learning cannot take the place of the inspiration of faith; statistics can never teach morals as forcibly as "Thus saith the Lord." More than this: statistics can never overturn the "Thou shalt not" of an Almighty God.

David has essayed to go forth to meet Goliath, well loaded down with Saul's armour, and David will meet with the defeat he deserves if he does not repent of the folly of matching such weapons against one who defies the armies of the living God. The warfare is a spiritual not a carnal one. What wonder that with such weapons courage has failed, the citadel is imperilled, and "counsels of despair" are urged. But these shall not prevail. That unrepentant soul shall not go unpunished by the wrath of a just God, who enters into complicity with the vice of fornication by consenting to the proposal for its State management.

But can this vice ever be actually exterminated? Probably never entirely by human law; but neither can stealing, so far as we are able to judge. The vice of stealing is likely to continue so long as the city of London exists, in spite of the most excellent human laws. Shall we then license stealing? No one who has a purse to be protected would advocate such rash legislation.

A conclusive answer to the plea of "a necessary evil" has been already given by our Judge. Looking upon the vices of those about Him, and the inevitable crop of increasing vice, with its attendant misery, to which his people were tending, He cried: "It must needs be that offences come; but," He added, "*woe to that man* by whom the offence cometh!" And shall we listen to proposals to set aside the sentence of Divine Justice for the tradition of men, and embody in human legislation the teaching, "It must needs be that offences come; but *peace* to that man by whom the offence cometh"? Let us rather, answer every specious array of misleading statistics, every false doctrine of medicine, every fresh cry of alarm, every blasphemous utterance against Christ's sufficient power to redeem, every infidel attack upon the sanctity of God's holy law, with the inexorable "Thou shalt not" of God's eternal commandment.

APPENDICES.

A. Fac-simile Reproduction of the Circular Memorandum issued by Lord Roberts.

B. Fac-simile of a Registration Ticket.

C. Letter To Lord George Hamilton.

APPENDIX A.

The photographic reduction of the following document was originally issued by the Friends' Association for Abolishing the State Regulation of Vice. It is here reproduced by their permission.

* * * * *

The Names of the Commander-in-Chief and of the Quartermaster-General who were in office on the date of issue of each of the Circular Memorandums mentioned in the following Parliamentary Return.

According to the Indian Army and Civil Service List, 1870 *to* 1876; *India List,* 1877 *to* 1886.

Date of Circular.	Commander-in - Chief.	Quartermaster-General.
20th July, 1870	LORD NAPIER of Magdala	COL. P. S. LUMSDEN.
20th November, 1871	Ditto	Ditto.
23rd August, 1872	Ditto	Ditto.
30th September, 1873	Ditto	Ditto or MAJOR-GEN. E. B. JOHNSON.
8th July, 1875	Ditto	COL. F. S. ROBERTS.
8th May, 1876	Ditto or SIR F. P. HAINES	MAJOR-GEN. F. S. ROBERTS.
19th August, 1876	SIR F. P. HAINES	Ditto.
28th February, 1878	Ditto	Ditto.
24th November, 1880	Ditto	—
23rd April, 1883	SIR D. M. STEWART	MAJOR-GEN. SIR C. M. MACGREGOR.
26th November, 1883	Ditto	Ditto.
12th July, 1884	Ditto	Ditto.
17th June, 1886	SIR F. S. ROBERTS	MAJOR - GEN. E. F. CHAPMAN.

On the 4th and 7th Aug., 1893, Lord Roberts disclaimed knowledge of the contents of the Circular Memorandum of June 17th, 1886 (see pages 63 and 84 of Parliamentary Return [C. 7148], of 1893). But on the 11th Aug., 1893, Lieut.-Gen. E. F. Chapman, who was Quartermaster-General at the time, gave very different evidence (see pages 85 to 90 of the same Return). He stated that Sir F. S. (now Lord) Roberts, the Commander-in-Chief, went on his usual cold weather tour of inspection in the early part of 1886, when he would have the fullest opportunity of consulting the general officers of his command on the subject. On his return to headquarters he discussed the matter with the Surgeon-General and the Quartermaster-General. The result of their deliberations was drawn up by the latter official, sent to Sir F. S. Roberts for his approval, and then issued by his authority to the subordinate military officials. A copy was sent to the Military Department of the Government of India for their information, and the receipt thereof acknowledged by them.

* * * * *

Fac-simile copy (reduced) of Lord Roberts' Circular Memorandum.
EAST INDIA (CONTAGIOUS DISEASES)

RETURN to an Address of the Honourable The House of Commons, dated 4 June 1888;—*for*,

"COPY of a CIRCULAR MEMORANDUM by the QUARTERMASTER GENERAL in India, dated 17th June 1886."

India Office, 4 June 1888.

J. A. GODLEY,
Under Secretary of State for India.

(Sir John Gorst.)

Ordered, by The House of Commons, *to be Printed, 4 June* 1888.

LONDON:
PRINTED BY HENRY HANSARD AND SON;
AND
Published by Eyre and Spottiswoode, East Harding-street, London, E.C., and 32, Abingdon-street, Westminster, S.W.; Adam and Charles Black, North Bridge, Edinburgh; and Hodges, Figgis, and Co., 101, Grafton-street, Dublin.

COPY OF A CIRCULAR MEMORANDUM BY THE QUARTERMASTER GENERAL IN INDIA, DATED 17TH JUNE 1886.

(No. 21.)

CIRCULAR MEMORANDUM.—Addressed to General Officers Commanding Divisions and Districts

Cantonment Lock Hospitals

Office of Quartermaster General in India,
Army Head Quarters, Simla,
17 June 1886.

Vide Précis of Circulars attached

In former years His Excellency the Commander in Chief has frequently impressed on General and Commanding Officers the necessity for adopting stringent measures to reduce the chances of venereal disease spreading more widely amongst the soldiers of the Army.

2. At the present time His Excellency desires me to give prominence to the following points which appear to be specially deserving of consideration by the Military and Medical authorities in every command.

The treatment of venereal disease generally is a matter calling for special devotion on the part of the medical profession.

To mitigate the evil now experienced, it is not only necessary to deal with the cases of troops in hospitals, but to arrange for a wider-spread effort which may reach the large centres of population, and, in this view, His Excellency has suggested to the Government of India the desirability of establishing a Medical School from which native practitioners trained in the treatment of venereal disease may be sent to the various towns throughout the country.

It can no longer be regarded as derogatory to the medical profession to promote the careful treatment of men and women who are suffering from a disease so injurious, and in mentioning the step which his Excellency has taken, he desires me to indicate the extreme importance in the first instance of medical officers being prepared to study and practice this particular branch of their professional work, under the assurance that their doing so must certainly result in the recognition of their efforts.

Whether or not the Lock Hospital system be extended, it is possible to encourage in every Cantonment, and in Sudder and Regimental Bazars, the treatment of those amongst the population who are suffering from venereal disease. The bulk of the women who practise the trade of prostitution are willing to subject themselves to examination by Dhais or by Medical Officers, if by their so doing they can be allowed to reside in regimental bazars.

Where Lock Hospitals are not kept up, it becomes necessary, under a regimental system, to arrange for the effective inspection of prostitutes attached to regimental bazars, whether in cantonments or on the line of march.

The isolation of women found diseased, and their maintenance while under treatment, becomes also a question to be dealt with regimentally.

In the regimental bazars it is necessary to have a sufficient number of women, to take care that they are sufficiently attractive, to provide them with proper houses, and above all to insist upon means of ablution being always available.

If young soldiers are carefully advised in regard to the advantage of ablution and recognise that convenient arrangements exist in the regimental bazar, they may be expected to avoid the risks involved in association with women who are not recognised by the regimental authorities.

The employment of Dhais, and insistance upon the performance of the acknowledged duties, is of great importance.

The removal of women who are pronounced to be incurably diseased from cantonment limits, should be dealt with as a police question in communication with the civil authorities.

In regard to the soldiers themselves, there are means at the disposal of Commanding Officers to enforce a more careful avoidance of contact with women who are diseased, where venereal is largely prevalent, the increase of the regimental police in controlling the movements of the men is imperative.

Frequent medical inspections should be ordered, and every endeavour should be made to make the men realize their own responsibility in assisting their officers, by indicating the women from whom disease has been acquired.

Much may be done to encourage a feeling amongst the men that it should be a point of honour to save each other where possible from risk in this matter.

The medical inspection of all detachments before leaving or entering a cantonment should be enforced by General Officers.

In conclusion, His Excellency desires me to impress upon all concerned the necessity for meeting the present difficulty by increased individual effort.

However much legislation may be desired to check the spread of disease, it is necessary to abandon a sense of false modesty in dealing with the matter in question, and to recognise that, as in the case of all other diseases, its open treatment, and the widespread knowledge of its disastrous effects, are the surest means of effacing it in each locality.

(By order)

E. F. Chapman, Major General,
Quartermaster General in India.

* * * * *

Précis of Circulars issued in the Quartermaster General's Department regarding the adoption of stringent Measures to reduce the chances of Venereal Disease spreading more widely amongst the Soldiers of the Army.

Number and Date of Circular.	PURPORT.
No. 43, dated 20th July 1870.	I. Officers commanding troops on the line of march to ensure the effective inspection of prostitutes attached to their regimental bazars. II. When any woman is found to be diseased, measures are to be adopted for her isolation on the march, and her transfer to the first or nearest Lock Hospital for treatment.
No. 87, dated 20th November 1871.	Forwards a copy of a report by the Sanitary Commissioner with the Government of India, reviewing the working of the rules for the prevention of venereal disease amongst British troops for the year 1870, and calls special attention to the necessity of officers commanding stations affording more efficient and energetic means for preventing the admission of casuals to the vicinity of the barracks. Any increase of disease should at once be met by increased energy on the part of Station and Regimental authorities, and especially of Regimental Police.
No. 51, dated 23rd August 1872.	Forwards copy of a communication from the Government of India to that of Bombay, regarding the disposal of incurable women attending Lock Hospitals, in which the former approves of a proposal to employ an incurable woman on small wages in the duties of the hospital at Mhow.
No. 80, dated 30th September 1873.	Directs that the practice of levying registration fees from prostitutes be discontinued.
No. 90, dated 8th July 1875.	Calls attention to Circular No. 87 of 1871, and strongly impresses upon Officers Commanding Divisions, Districts, and Stations, the necessity for strengthening the regimental police of corps when venereal is on the increase at a station, it being the general impression that the disease is not, as a rule, contracted from the registered women, but from unlicensed prostitutes who wander about the lines as hawkers, or are employed as coolies by the Public Works Department.

	2. Requests that it may be pointed out to regimental Commanders, and the Lock Hospital Sub-Committees, whose special duty it is to supervise the working of the Lock Hospital rules, how important it is that they should more actively exert themselves to check the prevalence of this disease.
No. 35, dated 8th May 1876.	The Commander in Chief in India having had under review the annual reports on the working of the Lock Hospitals at certain stations, His Excellency regrets to find that the results are not satisfactory when compared with those of previous years. 2. The Lock Hospital rules, as they stand, appear to meet all requirements, but it is considered that much greater vigilance and interest on the part of the local authorities is required for their efficient working. 3. The authorities most concerned in working out these rules are Commanding Officers of Regiments and Batteries, their Medical Officers, and the Sub-Committees, and their attention is called to the following points:— I. The number of women on the register is not in proportion to the number of men who visit them.
No. 35, dated 8th May 1876—*contd.*	II. The improvement of the conditions under which the women ply their trade, such as greater privacy, facilities for ablution, &c. &c. III. The kind treatment of the women and every reasonable inducement being held out to them to attend the Lock Hospital when suffering from disease. 4. Commanding Officers of regiments and batteries are to report at once to the General Officer Commanding, when any increase of venereal disease occurs amongst their men. Such reports to show the supposed causes of the increase, and the measures adopted for its suppression, and after remark by the Deputy Surgeon General to be forwarded to the Quartermaster General's Office. 5. The Lock Hospital Sub-Committee are to be assembled at least once a month, and their reports forwarded to General Officers Commanding.

	6. It is considered that a Careful attention to these points will contribute considerably towards checking the spread of venereal disease, and His Excellency hopes that no effort will be spared by either Regimental, Medical, or Local authorities to ensure more satisfactory results than have hitherto been obtained.
No. 67, dated 19th August 1876.	The annual reports on the working of Lock Hospitals during the year 1875, show that much venereal disease was contracted when on the line of march; Commanding Officers' attention should therefore be called to Circular No. 43 of 1870, and to the Medical Regulations which direct the Medical examination for venereal disease of every unmarried soldier on the day of his arrival at a new station from the line of march; and the effective inspection of the prostitutes accompanying the regimental bazars.
No. 11, dated 28th February 1878.	As it would appear that the great increase which prevails in a regiment on the line of march is attributable in a great measure to illicit prostitution, requests that the necessity for the exercise of greater care and vigilance on the line of march may be urged upon regimental authorities. 2. If necessary, some restriction should be placed on the men going out of camp, by posting picquets in different directions, and strengthening them when cases of venereal increase.
No. 68, dated 24th November 1880.	Draws attention to Circular No. 67 of 1876, and requests that the instructions therein contained regarding the medical examination of all unmarried soldiers on first arrival at a new station may be carried out, care being taken that the examination of the men is conducted with the utmost decency. 2. These medical examinations are of importance in detecting the existence and arresting the spread of venereal disease.
No. 23, dated 23rd April 1883.	Forwards for information and guidance an extract from a ruling of the Chief Court, Punjab, regarding the registration of women convicted of practising illicit prostitution.

No. 69, dated 26th November 1883.	The Commander in Chief requests that careful attention of Cantonment Committees and Lock Hospital Sub-Committees may be directed to the following points, wherever free quarters for registered women have been, or may hereafter be, established:— 2. Where cantonment funds can afford it, experienced and reliable Dhais should be employed to supervise the registered women.
No. 69, dated 26th November 1883—*continued.*	3. Such Dhais should be well paid if the fund can afford it, and they should be held responsible that:— I. The women under their charge consort with none but Europeans. II. That they do not entertain a man in any house but the one allotted them as quarters; III. That a woman is sent to hospital immediately she is found to be diseased; IV. To ensure the latter, the Dhai should examine the women daily between the periodical inspections of the medical officer. 4. Soldiers who have been diseased by registered women, have been frequently known to attribute it to women met in their walks outside the bazaar, and the diseased woman has thus been allowed to practise her trade in this state for sometime without detection. 5. Every house should therefore be numbered outside, or in some conspicuous spot inside, and a soldier on reporting himself sick should not be required to personally point out the woman from whom he contracted the disease, but merely to give the number of her house. 6. If the Dhai does her duty, these measures should lead to the early detection of disease amongst registered women. 7. Each house should be provided with a urinal and means of ablution, and such other preventive measures, within the means of the Cantonment Fund, as suggest themselves to local committees should be freely resorted to. 8. His Excellency will be prepared to sanction any reasonable expenditure from cantonment funds on the measures therein suggested.

No. 42, dated 12th July 1884.	Requests that the attention of Officers Commanding Stations may be drawn to the desirability when constructing free quarters for registered women, of providing houses that will meet the wishes of the women. 2. Unless their comfort and the convenience of those who consort with them is considered, the results will not be satisfactory.

APPENDIX B.

FAC-SIMILE OF A REGISTRATION TICKET OF EXAMINATION

Issued to a Prostitute in India, in 1892, notwithstanding the Resolution of the House of Commons of June 5, 1888, condemning such registration. The form employed is the one authorized by the East India Contagious Diseases Act of 1866, which was repealed in 1888.

1892

Ticket of Registered Prostitutes in the Cantonment of Meean Meer.—

Name. Begum 1st

Caste Mahamedan

Registered number. 1

Place of residence in Cantonment. Sudder Bazar

Date of Registry. 4—3—90

Personal appearance,

Offg. Cantonment Magistrate,
Meean Meer,

A. B. P., S. B., M. M.

3

Year and Month.	Date of Medical Examination and Signature of Medical Officer.				Remarks.
	Date of inspection in the 1st half month.	Signature of Medical Officer	Date of inspection in the second half month	Signature of Medical Officer.	
1892					
January ..	1-2-92		15.1.92 23.1.92 27.1.92	[illegible]	
February ...	1-2	[illegible]	15.1.92	[illegible]	
March ..					
April ..					
May ...					
June ...					
July ...					
August ...					
September,					
October ...					
November,					
December...					

APPENDIX C.

LETTER TO LORD GEORGE HAMILTON.

The following is the full text of the letter of retractation which Lady Henry Somerset addressed to Lord George Hamilton, January 27, as it appeared in the London daily papers of February 8, 1898:—

EASTNOR CASTLE, LEDBURY, *Jan.* 27, 1898.

DEAR LORD GEORGE HAMILTON,—Your lordship invited me ten months ago to give you my view of the dispatch that has been addressed to the Government of India on the health of the army, and in a letter in which I did so I ventured to suggest some methods, moral and disciplinary, which seemed to me the only ones likely to succeed, because they had at least the merit of being logical.

I was led to do so by two considerations: first, the dispatch in question seemed to imply that the Government would give every encouragement to every form of elevating agency, and so emphasize the altered spirit in which the subject was approached, and that such suggested supervision would only affect an incorrigible minimum; and second, that the system I had in mind would be so drastic and penal in its nature as to make State interference odious and finally impossible. That was ten months ago; and in that time nothing has been done of which the public has heard to strengthen the forces that make for moral improvement.

What has been done, viz., the repeal of the Indian Acts of 1895, which prohibited inspection, has been in a direction exactly opposite. It seems to have been the object of the Government to obtain the maximum of impunity, with the minimum of protest, from those who desire to see the State shape its actions according to Christian views of ethics. I need not tell your lordship I am not writing to say how strongly I am still opposed to the course which the Government has taken; but I find that my letter to your lordship of last year has been taken by many to mean that I am on the side of the accepted view of State regulation, and I am from time to time quoted as a sympathizer with such views. I am therefore writing to withdraw any proposals made in that letter for this reason—that the events of the past year have convinced me of the inadvisability and extreme danger of the system that in April last

I thought might be instituted.

The absence of any serious effort by the Government to bring about a higher standard in the army is a final proof to me that, as long as regulation of any kind can be resorted to as a remedy, it will always be regarded as the one and only panacea. My view was that it would be instituted as an odious but possibly effective auxiliary to moral efforts. I find it will always be accepted as a convenient substitute. I take the liberty of addressing this explicit withdrawal of an endorsement in whatever form of the principle of regulation; because it was in a letter to your lordship that I originally incurred the responsibility. I trust, therefore, to your lordship's indulgence to forgive me for troubling you further in the matter.—I remain, my lord, yours very truly,

(Signed) Isabel Somerset.

* * * * *

The following comments on the above letter appeared in *The Christian* (London), February 17, 1898:

REGULATION NO REMEDY.

In our last issue we inserted in full the letter of Lady Henry Somerset, in which she withdrew from her unfortunate position in relation to the State regulation of vice in India. We refrained, for the time being, from comment, that her retractation might speak for itself. We feel, therefore, the more free to remark upon it now.

We rejoice, in the first place, that it has come at all, for it justifies the principles for which we and other repealers have contended all these years. Lady Henry is convinced of "the inadvisability and extreme danger" of her former proposals, and recognises now that "as long as regulation of any kind can be resorted to as a remedy, it will be regarded as the one and only panacea . . . [and] will always be accepted as a convenient substitute [for moral reform]."

It is therefore with thankfulness that we note her ladyship's "explicit withdrawal of an endorsement in whatever form of the principle of regulation."

This is all good so far as it goes, but it does not go far enough; and, alas! it comes too late, for it can never undo the fearful harm her action last year was the means of doing.

A public retractation is a hard and painful process, and we sympathize with Lady Henry in the mental strain which it must have cost her. But she has not been the only sufferer. It were no small thing to cause division and discord in so gigantic an organization as that over which she presided, so that at the present time the movement is crippled and its machinery out of gear. This might well have elicited an expression of regret, which we hope may yet be forthcoming in some communication to the Association she has so grievously wronged.

But more than this. Encouraged by her act, the Government claimed the women of England as its supporters, defied moral sentiment, and, on the crest of the wave of this unhappy dissension, carried the re-enactment of the infamous C. D. Acts among our sisters in India. It will take long and weary years of uphill work to undo the mischief that her ill-advised and hasty action wrought. Meantime, how many Indian women will have succumbed to a shameful life and gone down to a dishonoured grave?

The weakest point of Lady Henry's letter is the erroneous assumption on which it is based: that her proposals themselves were moral, and that if the Government had instituted reforms they might have successfully co-existed with regulation. But how can regulation under any circumstances be a remedy? The very terms are self-contradictory. What is morally wrong can never be experimentally right, and this proposition neither casuistry nor expediency can set aside. The only remedy is obedience to the law of God; and if material aids be needed, let them be found in some active measures for the mental, moral, and spiritual improvement of our soldiers in their leisure hours. This is where reform is needed.

* * * * *

The foregoing Letter, together with the article from *The Christian,* were printed in full in *The Shield* (the official organ of the British Committee of the Federation for the Abolition of the State Regulation of Vice) of March, 1898, with the following

NOTE BY THE EDITOR.

"We are glad to see that Lady Henry Somerset has now withdrawn from the proposals for the Regulation of Vice with which her name has become connected. At the same time we regret that she still appears to think that her scheme could possibly have done good if side by side with it had been some moralizing agency. Our position is and has uniformly been that Regulation is essentially under all circumstances a demoralizing agency, and must be so from the very nature of the case; and that the provision of women certified fit for immoral purposes is necessarily disastrous whatever be the concomitants of such a proposition."

9 789361 387074

Printed by Libri Plureos GmbH in Hamburg,
Germany